FOREWORD

So many teachers work with children's singing voices and so few have had the opportunity to study age-appropriate pedagogy. Here is an ideal way to learn new skills and apply them directly to your work with young singers. There is an expertise in writing a book that is so straightforward, sensible and obvious; Dana Lentini has provided this from a depth of knowledge and years of experience. This book contains a balance of theoretical reasoning and practical solutions. Everything is explained and everything makes sense. The exercises are rich and diverse, and each one has a step-by-step guide through the process, making this easy to follow and implement in the teaching studio. Student-centered learning needs understanding and empathy; it needs respect for the young student who is capable of learning skills at an advanced level. Educating anyone needs a love of play and exploration to help them to discover these skills; the singer can learn how their joy of singing can be further enhanced and developed, and the teacher can know the right approach for each and every student. You will be extremely pleased to have this book!

Dr. Jenevora Williams PhD, ARCM
Author of Teaching Singing to Children and Young Adults, Compton Publishing Ltd.

TEACHING *the* CHILD SINGER

Pediatric Pedagogy for Ages 5–13

by Dana Lentini

Cover and interior photographs by Kelly Scaccia

ISBN 978-1-5400-4145-6

Visit Hal Leonard Online at
www.halleonard.com

Contact us:
Hal Leonard
7777 West Bluemound Road
Milwaukee, WI 53213
Email: info@halleonard.com

In Europe, contact:
Hal Leonard Europe Limited
42 Wigmore Street
Marylebone, London, W1U 2RN
Email: info@halleonardeurope.com

In Australia, contact:
Hal Leonard Australia Pty. Ltd.
4 Lentara Court
Cheltenham, Victoria, 3192 Australia
Email: info@halleonard.com.au

Dedication:
To all of my former, current and future students who continually inspire me
as we discover together the beautiful art of singing.

ACKNOWLEDGEMENT

My sincere thanks to Rick Walters for his commitment to publishing my work with the support of Brendan Fox at Hal Leonard. I am most appreciative of their knowledge, patience, and dedication that helped to complete this project. I am also indebted to Kristina Driskill at Gilded Within for her incredible wisdom, guidance, and for providing invaluable suggestions that helped to shape my thinking and writing. Thanks also to my friend and colleague Nikki Loney at Full Voice Music for her fantastic collaborations and incredible resources for teachers and their young singers. I am fortunate to have a friend and colleague in Jenevora Williams, whose in-depth research and dedication to furthering the science behind our understanding of the child singer have provided trusted advice and a kindred spirit in advancing the pedagogy outlined in my book. Heartfelt gratitude to my remarkable students and their parents through the years for providing me a landscape in which to inspire and create. I am truly grateful for the loving support of my husband and musician, Jim Lentini, for always believing in me and inspiring me to be my best, and to my three beautiful children who have taught me more than they will ever know. Finally, a special "thank you" to Fr. Ron Kurzawa and to Elizabeth Barrella, who both asked me at different stages of my life to look into my heart and see where I was being called. The results have been surprising, fulfilling, and wonderful.

TABLE OF CONTENTS

INTRODUCTION

Unleashing New Ideas from Old Traditions

Break Away from Conventional Thinking

Early in my teaching career, I would take calls from interested parents inquiring about voice lessons for their young children. I steered them away, because the conventional training I received as a singer and voice teacher did not prepare me to accept a variety of ages and stages in the singing lifespan. I was taught that children would ruin their voices if they took lessons, that they weren't old enough or mature enough to understand the sophistication involved in vocal technique, and that all children should be encouraged to study piano or violin instead. This generalized dismissal of the child singer left kids with no singing guidance, and stigmatized teachers who chose to work with young kids as being uninformed. But just as humanity has gained many new insights in other fields, effective ways of working with this young population have developed, and the conventional way of thinking no longer fits our modern understanding of how we can assist and support the child singer.

Imagine the possibilities—you get an email from a potential new student, and the parent explains that their five-year-old child loves singing in the car, at home, and school. The child is not interested in sports or studying an instrument; this little five-year-old wants to sing. Imagine you knew how to work with young children and were able to nurture their passion and love for singing. Imagine that children could learn beginning vocal technique and develop their musical talent along the way. Moreover, imagine a world where children aren't enchanted by developing mature musical tastes that are far beyond their years, but can listen and learn age-appropriate singing sounds. It is time to unleash new teaching strategies and break away from old stereotypes. This book is designed to start the dialogue of foundational singing techniques for children.

Where does a voice instructor begin to formulate new teaching methods if they haven't been exposed to such techniques? Indeed, most voice teachers are not equipped to teach young children. This book is designed to help voice instructors understand the many facets of working with pre-pubescent singers in the private voice studio and group singing classes. The reader will also gain a perspective as to why teachers, in recent years, have shied away from working with pre-adolescent singers in the private studio. This book will help shed light on the many myths and struggles that voice teachers have long been faced with when approached by eager parents and potential new students.

My Journey

As a lyric soprano with a performance degree and numerous stage credits, I was fortunate to gain extensive knowledge in pedagogy during my undergraduate performance degree. My courses were taught by a prominent pedagogue Dr. Thomas Cleveland, and were entrenched in the highly regarded lineage of William Vennard. While much of it was very scientific and thought-provoking, it left me enlightened and curious, as I matured and developed my own performance and teaching ideologies. Throughout the duration of my continued vocal studies and performing career, I began teaching voice lessons to high school students and avocational adults.

After several years of cultivating my dual singing and teaching career, I became a mom. During my years as a young mother, I found myself pursuing music lessons for my kids. It was then that I began forming my understanding of the many ways children can develop their musical talents. We started our oldest son on violin at age three. As a Suzuki parent, I realized that while my children were studying violin, they could have been learning to sing in this same technical grounding, but doing it with the instrument they were born with: the voice. We didn't need to rent or own an expensive violin or piano for them to develop their musical talents.

Why did we pick the violin? We had planned to start our oldest son on guitar, because my husband is a classical guitarist and composer. We had bought a child-sized guitar to get our son started. We always prided ourselves on the ways we exposed him to a variety of music, art, and culture. Somewhere he discovered the violin and all day long my little three-year-old was trying to put a giant guitar under his chin. He would use anything that resembled a stick or mallet to use as a bow. He was obsessed with the violin. As we thought about his future guitar studies, my husband and I decided that maybe his current passion for the violin would be the better option to start his formal music lessons. If a child is showing an interest or has a passion, why not act on it? We were intrigued by this desire and decided to give it a try. One thing I have learned as a parent: children can be very stubborn. You know the old saying: "You can lead a horse to water, but you can't make him drink." If a child loves to sing, they will sing. It does not serve them to offer piano lessons or other instrumental lessons if it is not what they want.

Many people believe that children should not begin formal singing lessons until the voice has matured and suggest piano should be a child's first instrument of study. I now advocate that the singing voice can be a child's first introduction to musical study, especially if the child shows an interest in singing. Many children love to sing and are inspired by performing songs. I agree that piano and stringed instruments are beneficial to musical literacy, but why should we only offer those lessons as a foundation in musical study? Young children don't have fully grown hands to fit on the standard piano keys, and yet they can still learn to play piano. Children taking voice lessons can certainly be encouraged to study piano or another instrument in addition to the vocal studies. They might even be more inspired to do so once they have gained a love for independent music study based on their passion for singing. The old school of thought that the piano should come first is not always the best option. I had several students start voice lessons with me when they were five or six and later add piano lessons, in addition to their vocal studies. I have nurtured their love for singing, which in turn motivated them to dig deeper into their musical studies. Why is it that so many think it should be the other way around? Let's ignite their passion before it fades out, and we lose them to sports. If voice lessons are what they want, voice lessons they should get.

Fresh Outlook

As my family grew, we moved out of state and new opportunities came my way. I had to establish my teaching methods and studio in a new locale. I was offered an adjunct teaching position at a college teaching studio voice, courses in vocal pedagogy, and group singing classes for music majors. While teaching at the college, I had also accepted an elementary school teaching position, something I never imagined myself doing. I have always kept a positive outlook and have allowed myself to see the many possibilities that come next. Before accepting the teaching position, I had experience directing a children's choir at my church, which was another opportunity that had presented itself to me without warning. Directing a children's choir wasn't exactly how I had envisioned my career path, but it was a great experience and guided me tremendously in the classroom.

It was these combined adventures that led to my ideas and teaching philosophies I now hold in my heart when working with young children. Being open-minded and staying current with trends always helps me welcome new possibilities and opportunities. You could say that I am a person who strives to uncover truths and enjoys challenges. One of the myths I wanted to uncover as a voice teacher is; why are there so many biases regarding young children in the private studio, and why do voice teachers shy away from teaching them?

Most teachers do not know how to teach young singers because no one ever taught them and they have never worked with kids. Most teachers are not aware of the physical differences in the pre-pubescent larynx. There are still many who believe that teaching this age is dangerous, because they do not have an understanding of how the voice works. Some teachers just do not enjoy working with young children, and that is fine. One of the biggest reasons, however, that voice teachers cringe at children studying voice, is the exploitation of kids' singing on TV in talent shows, with audiences being wowed by little children singing and sounding like grown-ups. This popular promotion can cause anger and frustration among voice teaching experts. This has led some parents to advocate for their children as a result of their own agenda. It is not fair, however, to assume that all voice teachers working with young children are training their pre-adolescent singers to be media sensations any more than one might assume piano and violin teachers are grooming their students for the sole purpose of fame and fortune. It is also not fair to assume that all parents are pursuing voice lessons for their children because they want them to be in the spotlight. Some well-intentioned parents and families are interested in pursuing voice lessons by the simple fact their children love to sing, and these families want to feed their child's curiosity while cultivating a growth mindset. Music lessons, of any discipline, should be taught from the standpoint that a well-rounded education, including study in the arts, helps develop emotional and intellectual character.

New Beginnings

I came to develop my expertise in working with children singers after I taught at the elementary school. Teaching in the classroom was a love-hate relationship, mostly because classroom instruction in an elementary school was not where my talents flourished, and working within the "song-approach" methodology frustrated me. I saw that many children loved to sing, and I realized they could easily gain more formalized singing training with the correct procedures. Instead of just going through the motions of singing songs, I began supplementing my classes with solo singing techniques. Along the way, I discovered my enjoyment in nurturing their singing curiosity.

After several years in the classroom, another new job opportunity moved our family halfway across the country. This new location led me away from the college setting and out of the elementary school classroom, and into a new scenario of voice teaching. I decided to start a large group voice class for children at my local community arts center. I based the course around my recent experiences on the school curriculum that I had devised and developed a five-step system. I established the singing methods on a combined ideology from my college voice courses I taught and the elementary classroom procedures I modified. What resulted was a hybrid voice class for children based on the cultivation of singing and performing techniques. The class was called Born 2 Sing Kids. The first class I hosted included twelve children, and the next session enrolled eighteen students. It was a wonderful, diverse group of eager young singers of various ages and backgrounds. I refined and created the Born 2 Sing Kids Five-Step System for my large group classes and I began to see the amazing results.

After several years of successfully teaching children singing, my husband's career path evolved, and I had to move yet again. However, in every new place, I looked for ways to cultivate my skills and interests.

That move landed me in the perfect situation to broaden my knowledge and get back to the hunger that had begun in my early college years, seeking more in-depth expertise in vocal pedagogy. After all those years of working with children, I was intrigued to know more about their unique qualities. I was not able to find any information on why there are so many myths surrounding pediatric vocal pedagogy, and why no one educates voice teachers on the different skills required to work with young children in the private studio. Of course, universities offer degrees in music education that focus on the aspects of working with children in the classroom, but what I wanted was information about vocal pedagogy relating to solo singing and performing for the pre-pubescent singer. It is encouraging that there is so much research going on worldwide about voice science. Voice teachers in the twenty-first century are gaining great strides in the understanding of how the voice works, from the physics of sound and vocal technique, to the understanding of performance anxiety and work with transgender voices. Through these discoveries, we are gaining groundbreaking information, but not enough resources exist yet for understanding these distinct differences in children. In the quest to know more, I found myself back in the classroom.

Emerging through my years of teaching, singing, and raising my family, I decided to enroll in a master's degree program with a concentration in vocal pedagogy. Being a college student in middle age was humbling and challenging. Learning the latest technology for the classroom was enough to scare me away, but I was determined, and the benefits were tremendous. I was able not only to pursue a degree in vocal pedagogy, but also to concentrate my personal research goals of teaching methodologies and ideologies for the pre-pubescent singer. I set out on a journey to find out who was working with children and what data and research there was to back up any claims about the negative criticism circling singing lessons for this young age group. I continued to learn, grow, and study from other experts in my unique area of pediatric pedagogy, but mostly I learned from my continued work with my young voice students. Even today, I still advance in my knowledge by taking careful notes and watching the learning, growing, developing, and nurturing that takes place every week in the studio, as these earnest little singers discover the art of beautiful singing and musicianship. My joy is empowering young singers one lesson at a time.

Connecting the Dots

During my time teaching singing to children in the group setting, I began to realize the immense potential and ability of a private lesson scenario. Through the years, though, I was still stuck in the old ways of thinking. I believed in that nagging allegation that kids should not take private voice lessons. It continually evokes debate and scrutiny among many singing experts. In my younger teaching days, I joined in on that philosophy. Since I was never trained or taught how to work with children in the private studio, I didn't understand the unique qualities or attributes that might coincide with pediatric vocal pedagogy. I wasn't yet connecting the dots that if I could work with singers in a choir, classroom, or group setting, why couldn't I teach them in the voice studio? Even when I was teaching solely the group classes and prospective parents approached me about private lessons for their young child, I would commonly shoo them away and say that young singers should wait until they were more mature, typically around the age of thirteen, to start formal voice lessons. The middle school years seem to be more suitable because this is when adolescence begins, and the young larynx has physically grown to its adult size. Physical growth becomes more advanced, along with cognitive and mental maturity. Beyond the level of development, however, I would often wonder why it is that most voice teachers do not feel compelled to take on younger singers. The truth is, I didn't know what to do with a child in the private studio. Typical voice lesson pacing is certainly not conducive to young children standing and singing for 30-60 minutes at a time. I came to an understanding that most voice teachers are trained primarily in the old school methodology of the "master-apprentice model."

The Master-Apprentice Model

The master-apprentice learning and teaching model, as described by Jessica O'Bryan and Scott D. Harrison in the book *Teaching Singing in the 21st Century*, began in Europe in the late Middle Ages. From this time into the late nineteenth century, young singers were apprenticed for not only their vocal and musical training but also their moral and physical development. As vocal training developed throughout Europe, other teaching models became prominent, and in certain regions, class and group training became the typical scenario. Singers worked with a "master-teacher" who was regarded as the authority for young and emerging artists. Vocal education evolved into the twentieth century, with conservatories becoming the training grounds for young adult musicians.

The conservatory model still sets the standard structure of a voice lesson in our modern culture. The current lesson scenario for most adult voice lessons follows a curriculum of vocalizing followed by repertoire work, but this structure becomes very problematic when working with children. Addressing pacing and voice lesson structure sheds light on how singing lessons for all ages can and should include a well-rounded study of musical and vocal training.

Learning from a master teacher and forming teaching strategies based on one's learning model narrows ideas for a variety of method practices. This model limits the teacher to only strategize based on what they have learned in their own voice lessons established around their individual needs. My training as a singer was in the same scenario. In college, everything I had learned about singing was from my voice teachers. Once I started immersing myself in the technical aspects of singing, I gained more knowledge about techniques in my pedagogy courses. But these courses focused primarily on the physical mechanism of the laryngeal structure and how to diagnose and correct vocal faults in the adult singer. While I was gaining insight into pedagogy from a scientific point of view, I was still not well versed in lesson pacing practices. I set out teaching voice lessons in the same manner in which I learned singing based on the conservatory master-apprentice model. Since I did not start studying singing when I was a child, I did not discover any skills from personal experience on how to pace a lesson or teach vocal procedures to pre-pubescent voices.

Repertoire Approach

There is a lack of academic training available in higher education that offers comprehensive knowledge in the field of pediatric vocal pedagogy. Voice teachers looking to provide singing lessons for children have limited opportunities for formal training on the topic. For this reason, interested child singers and their parents can find it challenging to locate a qualified teacher who has pedagogical expertise. Some teachers who work with young singers do not have formal training in the area of pediatric vocal pedagogy. Many teachers currently working with children apply a teaching style centered around the "repertoire" approach. This results in students merely learning to sing songs focusing on the performance aspect, with little or no attention to the physical awareness of technique.

During the twentieth century, conservatories flourished in the cultivation of classical singing. At the same time, methods for teaching children progressed in a different direction. In his book *Teaching Kids to Sing*, Kenneth Phillips gives historical information on the development of pedagogy for young singers and the advancement of the "song-approach" for teaching singing that began in the first half of the twentieth century. This ideology led to enhancements for the classroom singer and the choral singer. As this became the focus, Dr. Phillips points out that the vocal technique of the young solo singer suffered, primarily because of the desire for "straight tone" singing to achieve the choral blend.

In the second half of the twentieth century, the music curriculum of the American education system was transformed by different teaching methods from other countries. Zoltán Kodaly from Hungary, Carl Orff from Germany, and Émile Jaques-Dalcroze from Switzerland all brought new-found methodologies for teaching music skills. The methods they incorporated did not focus on the technique and mastery of the singing voice but continued the "song" approach to singing, which has continued into the twenty-first century. While all of these methods are musically enriching, they still lack attention to comprehensive vocal technique.

Voice teachers working with children need to know the technical aspects of developmental success. Impressionable children can and do develop poor singing techniques, especially in the form of over-singing. Children studying singing in the hands of an uninformed teacher can indeed cause harm by over-singing. The result is an impression that voice lessons for kids are risky, causing potential damage to their growing voices. Still, on the contrary, kids can learn good singing strategies and achieve wonderful results by studying singing with a well-informed voice teacher who knows the field of pediatric pedagogy.

Bloom and Grow

While I derive happiness from working with young children, I am also inspired by moderating group engagement on social media, blogging, and collaborating with other voice teachers at conferences and workshops. It is encouraging to share passions and spread the knowledge that working with children is as rewarding for the students as it is for the teachers. One key factor is that it furthers the advancement of healthy and beautiful singing practices to the world of singing as a whole. Children are born ready to use their voice. As they develop through childhood, they use their voice to communicate in a variety of ways. If voice teachers begin the groundwork with young children regarding healthy singing techniques, imagine the potential for changing the landscape of artful and healthy singing as they grow and develop. A good foundation leads to less vocal injury and more efficient singing. Like planting seeds that eventually grow into a firmer foundation, young singers can continue to grow and carry with them into adulthood the many wonders of singing and song literature.

Many parents have gone on to praise not only their children's ability to perform but the confidence they have gained when taking singing lessons. My solution to many of the pitfalls when working with children lands in the lesson pacing found in the five-step system, which will be explained later in this book. The organized curriculum has proven to be successful by giving me the tools I need to direct the content and the principle behind what I am teaching. Further testimonials I have received from parents and kids have confirmed that teaching children in the proper techniques of singing are far-reaching. They praise not only the technical abilities gained from using a systematic approach, but also the benefits in other areas of child development, including emotional and academic progress.

In her book *The Evolving Singing Voice*, Karen Brunssen (2017, p. 6) points out, "At every age, exercising the singing voice regularly increases the elasticity of the muscles of breathing and the larynx." We must start children off on the right path to good singing habits so that the foundation of these singing muscles are developing properly. In this book, I lay out the research we know so far about the physical and mental differences that children bring to voice lessons. I also explain the ideas and teaching strategies I employ in the private studio, and in my small and large group classes. Take these ideas and strategies and build on them to create your own methods and ideas. When there is a planned course of action there is better chance for success.

SECTION 1

How is teaching a child different from teaching an adult or teen singer?

CHAPTER 1:
Children Are Not Mini-Adults

Meet each student where they are and gently guide them to a better place, allowing growth and art to flourish.

As explained in the introduction, the "master-apprentice" model, which has inspired the current voice lesson structure, does not adequately prepare an instructor when working with children. The voice teacher needs to understand how young singers require a different environment, set of expectations, and mindset. Children working in the private studio need a lesson structure to serve their unique needs. Many voice teachers believe that lesson structure should be different by merely making it a mini-voice lesson, shortening the time frame down to thirty or fifteen minutes to accommodate shorter attention spans. But children are not smaller versions of adult voice students and need more than just a shortened voice lesson. They are growing and changing and have special learning needs. Gaining knowledge to teach a variety of age groups can enhance a studio teacher's pedagogy expertise. It is essential for a good teacher to be adaptable and flexible, adjusting teaching strategies for individual singers of all ages. As instructors, we cannot expect all of our students, young or old, to meet our qualifications and fit to a mold. In the voice studio, each singer comes to lessons with a variety of skill sets and maturity level, and may progress at a different rate. A good teacher must be able to meet each student where they are and to gently guide them to a better place, allowing growth and art to flourish. To do this, we must first understand the differences a child singer possesses.

There are many physical differences with the young growing instrument. In her book *Teaching Singing to Children and Young Adults*, author Jenevora Williams (2013, pp. 25-29) lays out the distinct differences in the child's vocal mechanism. The larynx, colloquially referred to as the "voice box," is a part of the growing body. Before puberty sets in, the larynx has a different shape, length, and structure than the adult counterpart. An important distinction regarding children is that the larynx is higher in the neck and sits closer to the back of the jaw. This results in a smaller area in which sound can resonate, higher pitch frequencies, and brighter tone quality. In general, the child's larynx is softer and rounder before puberty, and as a consequence, the execution for singing will be less intense and not as loud or agile. The layers of the vocal folds themselves are also not fully intact and are shorter and thinner before puberty. Thus, a child's vocal range is not as big and flexible as an adult's. Finally, a child has smaller lung capacity, so long phrases and breath-pressure for stabilizing sound are not as fully developed as that of an adult. The expectations of long and flexible phrases or scales should be avoided for children, because the child's physical mechanism is not suited to this type of musical execution. The repertoire that includes this kind of singing should be bypassed until the student advances into these skills with time and maturity.

In my observation of the beginning solo child singer, I have found the average comfortable vocal range is about middle C (C4) to about G5 (two Gs above middle C).

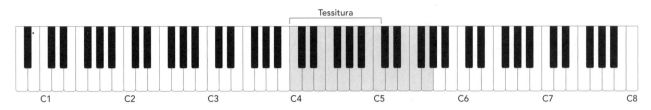

Of course, some children come with skill sets that far exceed this, or are not quite there yet, but the average can be expected. The vocal range where a song should comfortably lie is not necessarily the range in which a young singer can vocalize from high to low. Many child singers can vocalize utilizing more than a two-octave range, but the average tessitura of vocal ease is within the range of C4-C5. Working with children who have expansive range to their voice doesn't always mean that they can or should sing utilizing that capacity. Many children need to work on balancing registers and gain flexibility before they can adequately sing repertoire with an extensive vocal range.

As a voice starts to approach pre-pubertal changes, young singers can begin to lose some of their ability to sustain the higher pitches. Working recently with a boy-soprano age 12, who auditioned for the lead in *Amahl and the Night Visitors,* proved that range does not constitute stamina in a particular tessitura. This student was encouraged to audition because the director knew he had a high range that could extend beyond the typical child's vocal expectations. Once we worked on the score, it was easy to see that it didn't matter how high he could sing, but how well he could execute the bulk of the singing range. The tessitura for the role of *Amahl* sits around the top of the staff between D5-F5. It also requires light singing in that range. The general tessitura of that role was most unsuitable for this young singer's changing voice. In addition, casting a pre-pubertal boy in a role of this nature could become problematic with further voice change during the rehearsal and performance period. Fortunately, my student did not get the role, which was a blessing for his emerging and changing voice. If he had been cast in the role, he would have undergone overuse and abuse of his growing voice, trying to fit into something that he had outgrown. Singing outside of one's comfort zone can be problematic for a mature and full-grown singer, of course, and it certainly would have been detrimental for a young, evolving voice.

When working with children, the instructor must be knowledgeable in the distinctive qualities of the growing instrument and have the resources to facilitate this expertise. Voice teachers working individually with pre-pubescent singers must understand these physical differences to avoid misuse. As stated previously, children are not merely smaller versions of their adult counterparts, they are special, and require their own pedagogy. There are limits for children concerning pitch range, flexibility, loudness, and stamina. Establish an adaptable and flexible environment where singing is understood and kept in moderation for children. Teachers of young singers are keeping guard over these blossoming voices.

CHAPTER 2:
The Growing Treble Voice

Start them on the right path to good singing habits.

Voice registration and vocal range are some of the first things a teacher observes at an initial voice lesson with an adult student. For mature classical singers, voice classification guides the type of repertoire the student cultivates. For children in the voice lesson, it is not necessary to classify a young singer based on voice type. Although a child's range should be evaluated early for monitoring progress, it is not the first observation for repertoire cultivation. All pre-pubescent singers are regarded as treble voices. This is because of their high, light quality and pitch range. Young males do not have the range of tenor or bass yet. The term "treble" refers to the highest voice part in a choir, and in the sacred choral tradition, it is an unchanged boy's voice. Both boys and girls sing in the same vocal range and both should be able to easily access the head and chest voice registers and can equally sing the same repertoire before puberty sets in.

An initial observation with a student should determine if a child understands head voice quality, or CT dominant singing. CT dominant singing refers to the action of the cricothyroid adjustment of the larynx that creates what most teachers refer to as head voice singing (meaning that the vocal folds are vibrating lightly, and with less contact). Not all children can easily access the higher and lighter quality of their treble voice. Remember that a child's average voice range is between C4 and G5. Within that range, they can sing in a light tone quality for the higher notes (head voice or CT dominant) and a darker and heavier timbre in the lower half of the range, which is referred to as chest voice—or TA thyroarytenoid dominant (thicker parts of the vocal folds vibrating with more intense contact). For clarity in this book I will use "head voice" and "chest voice" to describe these two registers.

There are a few reasons why most young singers have a hard time finding what is generally described as head voice. Children and adults commonly speak in the lower part of their vocal range closer to middle C. This type of phonation is produced in a chest voice quality. Singing with a lighter voice feels awkward to many unaccustomed to this sensation. Children exposed to lots of popular music are inspired by the singing styles that incorporate heavy singing sounds. This influence is another reason that many singers, young and old, struggle to find lighter singing resonance. Getting children involved with lessons at an earlier age, before specific characteristics and bad habits set in, can have a very influential impact. Singers need to gain a conceptual understanding of registers before they overuse or misuse their young and growing instruments. A child can and should learn the different ways of producing good tone and should be able to discern which one feels comfortable and efficient. If a child is stuck only using the chest voice registration and struggles to find a lighter resonance, they will often display a variety of issues, including pitch-matching problems, and have minimal vocal range.

Imitating Adult Singers

Finding passion for singing often comes from listening and observing, but it is important to help young singers find their own true sound. Many children come to voice lessons because they are influenced by a particular genre or artist. Through my years of teaching I have seen how these influences in vocal style have evolved. In recent years the commercial music styles have had a huge impact on the way young girls emulate their singing sounds. I had a young student, Amanda, aged 10, who was stylish and talented. She was quite inspired by pop culture at large and admired her favorite singer, Christina Perri. Every song she sang was infused with the style and mannerisms she learned from her idol. At her first lesson she sang for me one of Perri's hit songs. Amanda pulled off all of the nuances and made many attempts to sound just like the pop star. While I think it can be inspiring for a young singer to emulate their idol, I don't think it is necessarily the best model for singers to try and fit into one particular mold. Amanda was not able to produce tone in an efficient manner for her voice. She struggled to find most of the notes and strained her voice in the process. There is a huge age difference between many young students and their pop idols. Trying to imitate can result in vocal misuse, which leads to abuse and vocal injury.

There is also a current trend to use an excessive amount of "vocal fry" (suppressing the larynx to produce a low-pitched creaky sound). This technique has weaved its way into everyday speech for many young girls. Vocal fry can lead to problems as the voice matures and has been a known contributor to voice pathology. Amanda applied vocal fry sounds into every song she sang. It was also beginning to creep into her speech patterns. In the first year we worked together, we spent most of our time freeing up the voice, locating her head voice register, and discovering her unique sound. Once she developed an ability to phonate in her head voice, she had a more capacity of range and possibilities. It is fair to say that young singers can and will still sing along with, and model their favorite singers, but they should gain a variety of skills and understand how their voice works best.

Puberty and Voice Change

Keeping efficiency and flexibility a priority for young singers will help them as they grow and evolve through childhood. As the singer develops through puberty, the vocal folds grow, and the range expands to include an extension of higher and lower notes. An unchanged boy's voice generally has the same pitch range as his female counterparts. It isn't until after puberty sets in that the voices have different qualities and attributes.

Puberty is unique and makes many changes to the vocal mechanism. These changes will often present challenges for the voice teacher and student. Singing teachers working with children need to be aware of the many adjustments that can occur. As previously explained, the size and length of the young larynx and vocal folds are proportionately different by size and placement during childhood. Dr. Jenevora Williams points out in her book the age of onset for pubertal changes has been falling worldwide (2013, p. 57). Children today are starting puberty earlier than they did in the past. She goes on to explain how the duration of these puberty changes can last from only a few months up to four years. In a recent interview with Dr. Williams, she told me that it is essential for the voice teacher to prepare young singers in advance for the changes—in both boys and girls—that are to come. Having knowledge and empathy for pre-pubescent singers can help ease the transition and guide them through the many transformations that will take place.

As the child goes through adolescence, this change starts to take root as the vocal instrument grows to its adult dimensions. It is during this growth that boys and girls develop differently. For girls, the change can begin around age 10–12, and for boys, it is on average closer to age 13. Of course, this is just a general rule of thumb as every individual is unique and has

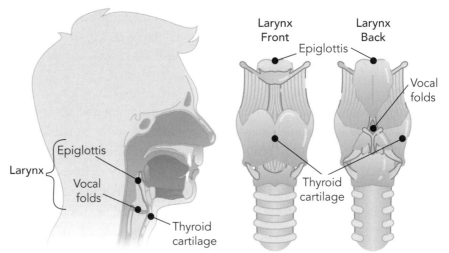

certain qualities that are not always the norm. Some boys' voices can change at age 11, and others not until 14 or 15 or later. It is during this time of change that the larynx grows in size, length and strength. The mutational shift that takes place is most evident in the thyroid cartilage. The thyroid is shaped like a shield and is the largest of the three cartilages that make up the larynx. The male thyroid grows from front to back and the vocal folds will lengthen with about a 60% increase in length. Since the larynx grows from front to back it causes the prominence of the "Adam's apple." The boy's vocal folds grow not only in length, but thickness, as well, and this is why there is such a dramatic change in vocal quality. Thicker vocal folds mean lower frequencies, thus rendering lower pitches (Williams, 2013, p 61).

The Boy's Changing Voice

Boys go through several stages during this change and some considerations should be made for each stage of a young man's transition. There are several theories and books written on the topic of the changing male voice, but the Cambiata approach and the Cooksey system are the most modern and widely accepted schools of thought.

The Cambiata Concept was introduced by Irvin Cooper and Don Collins as a way to manage the changing male voice. The term "cambiata" literally means "change." In this approach, there are four types of boys' voices through which a young man will transition. The first stage is the unchanged treble voice, the second stage is the "cambiata" or changing voice, the third stage is the baritone I voice, and in the last and fourth stage, the boy's voice enters into a deeper more resonant baritone II voice. In their approach, Cooper and Collins believe that the true tenor voice emerges later in a young man's twenties (Phillips, 1996, p. 79).

The Cooksey System, also referred to as the Contemporary Eclectic Approach, was introduced by John Cooksey shortly after the Cambiata Concept. In this methodology, Mr. Cooksey has a contrasting strategy and recognizes a different set of phases for the male voice change. Both of these methods, Cooksey and Cambiata, offer a great understanding of what a young man is experiencing and how to navigate this exclusive stage (Phillips, 1996, p. 80).

My student who auditioned for *Amahl and the Night Visitors* was most definitely in the second phase of his "cambiata" voice. Though he still had most of his range, he lost the light and agile quality in his higher tessitura to qualify him as an alto rather than a high soprano, which is what the role of *Amahl* requires. This is what made his singing for the role very difficult. Since the voice can change without notice and can happen in an instant, it is advised to be careful when a changing voice is cast in a role that could demand the singer to stay in a strict vocal range that may be comfortable during auditions, but that with a voice change could become too demanding or uncomfortable come opening night. In the private studio, it is not essential for the teacher to agonize over the voice change for fear of having an unbalanced ensemble the way it is for a conductor. These Cambiata and Cooksey categories are mostly helpful for choir directors to use as guidelines. In the private studio, the voice teacher has much more freedom to allow the young male voice to emerge without hindrance. When working with a student going through this change, it is advised to keep record of where the range is from week to week. Keep tabs on not only how high and how low the singer is able to go in each weekly lesson, but also keep tabs on where the easiest tessitura lies.

During pubertal changes, it is imperative to continue teaching technical strategies regarding posture, breath and the avoidance of straining. These are essential areas of focus. In choosing repertoire, I personally keep boys singing in their lower tessitura so as not to create tension or bad habits from reaching for the higher pitches. At the beginning of a lesson, I like to start off our warm-ups by having the young male singer speak backward the numbers from 20 and sustain the spoken pitch on the final number to discern where the optimal speaking pitch level is located. Once we find that pitch, I go up an octave and have him sing a do-sol-do glide on /u/. My technical approach to vocal warm-ups is "top-down," having a singer work their top voice first and then work our way down into the lower range. With that, I'll let a boy sing where he feels most comfortable without taking him to the highest point in his vocal range where he is straining. Avoiding tension and overtaxing is of utmost attention. It is helpful to know the individual range guidelines when choosing solo repertoire for a boy going through a vocal change. This can be challenging and the teacher should be prepared to transpose keys at any given moment should changes occur, while learning a piece.

The Girl's Changing Voice

Puberty for girls is different and not as impactful. Girls grow at a different rate, and the female vocal folds will increase by about 34% in length (Williams, 2013, p. 61). The growing female larynx is not as striking and grows more in height than in width. This non-linear growth has an overall effect on girls by causing breathiness. The breathiness is caused by weaker adductor muscles (these muscles draw the vocal folds together) at the back of the vocal folds. It is essential to understand that this is normal and will improve with age and maturity. A teacher should be cautioned by over-correcting breathiness in a lesson, as it can cause ill effects. This breathiness is a natural progression during puberty. Girls can also be affected by the onset of their monthly cycle, which at this young age can vary in regularity. The delicate tissues of the vocal folds can suffer inflammation as a result of water retention. During this time, a young girl can also be affected by cramps and general discomfort.

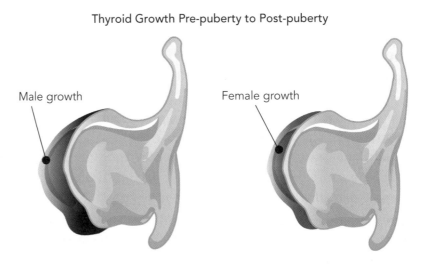

Thyroid Growth Pre-puberty to Post-puberty

Male growth

Female growth

The Treble Voice

Even before puberty sets in, children can have a difficult time finding their own authentic voice and how to discern the registers. Children should not be classified in their voice lessons by voice type or part. Instead, describing children's voices as "treble," is a better way to describe unchanged voices. Children can lack the ability to consistently match pitches or sing in the correct range of a song or exercise. I have found this problem primarily related to the understanding and ability to create vibration in the head voice mechanism. As I already mentioned, the head voice register is a result of the vocal folds vibrating more lightly with less contact. Head voice feels unnatural for many young girls, but it is also incredibly awkward for boys who find that it is not a strong or masculine sound. Teachers can assist by working with the head voice mechanism away from the piano and in songs. Instead of discovering head voice while singing, I recommend creating light and high sounds by having the singers read poetry or short stories using different pitch exploration in speech. This can take the fear or awkwardness away and allow singers to discover through play using fun and creative sounds.

Teachers working with children need to find songs and repertoire that suit the vocal range for growing treble voices. Repertoire needs to be chosen with smaller vocal ranges than you would prescribe for an older more advanced student. Even with children who have tremendous talent and ability to sing outside of the norm, it is always necessary to remember that intensity and duration of singing should be kept in moderation to avoid overuse or abuse to protect the delicate tissues of the growing and maturing instrument.

CHAPTER 3:
Unique Learning and Vocal Care for Kids

Create a relaxed environment and allow their unique personality to reflect in their art.

Emotional Development

Children are different not only in their individual physical characteristics, but also in their emotional and cognitive abilities. Recognizing that children need specific pedagogy, it is essential for the voice teacher to understand the individuality and temperaments that children display in the studio. All of the various ages and stages that children go through as they grow and mature can present new challenges to a voice lesson each week.

Throughout childhood, kids will evolve through these different areas of development:

- **Cognitive skills:** Children will go through various stages as they enhance their capacity for thinking, learning, and problem-solving.

- **Social and emotional skills:** Children are learning and growing in the many ways they relate to other people. These skills include how they express and control their emotions, which is a contributing factor for understanding vocal expression.

- **Speech and language skills:** Young children are cultivating their ability to understand language and communication. They are gaining knowledge of vocabulary and progressing in speech sounds.

- **Fine and gross motor skills:** Kids are developing small muscle groups (fine motor skills), and large muscles (gross motor skills) in the body.

- **Life skills:** The ability to gain independence and responsibility.

Learning Differences

In addition to their maturation levels concerning emotional and cognitive skills, children today are recognized in school with different abilities concerning learning and attention issues. A voice teacher should possess understanding for each student and be aware of these unique differences to determine the best approach for growth. A child may be receiving special services at school and is usually evaluated and diagnosed by a professional service provider regarding specific learning and attention issues. Many of these children can gain valuable experiences from formal voice lessons. When a child who struggles in school is recognized as having musical talent, this unique ability can boost confidence and pride. Voice lessons and group singing classes should be a place of inclusion for all types of learners.

When understanding the variety of learning issues, it is best if a teacher does not address the issue directly with the singer. A child in the voice studio needs to be recognized as a musician and not labeled as a child with specific learning challenges. The voice teacher should have empathy for all students and use the following information about learning differences as a way of gaining new perspectives and teaching strategies for all children. A well-informed teacher who is mindful of specific issues. Noticing how each child is an individual helps a teacher plan and set personal objectives for all types of learners. Understanding the various types of learning and attention differences will aid the teacher in lesson planning and pacing. Do not label any child as different. Each singer is unique, and these specific qualities are what make a truly gifted artist. Create a relaxed environment and allow a child's unique personality to reflect in her or his art.

Outlined here are a few examples of learning and emotional issues that can affect a child. Understanding these attributes can help a teacher relay information on a different level or allow more time for a student to grasp a concept.

- **ADHD** can cause a child to need more patience from a teacher. Lack of attention and focus can create different symptoms for various ages and stages. Some children will show signs of hyperactivity and impulsivity in a lesson. A student who has attention difficulty requires a very organized lesson structure and well-organized practice assignments. Later in the book, we will cover strategies to help direct this behavior with structured lesson activities.

- **Dysgraphia** is difficulty with writing legibly and putting thoughts down on paper. Allow these children more time in a lesson to complete writing tasks and assign less demanding work, so they do not become overwhelmed.

- **Speech Delays** can cause a student to need more time with enunciation goals and articulation within a song. If a student is not making normal progression in their speech development, and it is causing disturbances in the lessons, the voice teacher should consider making a recommendation to seek outside help from a trained Speech-Language Pathologist (SLP). Voice lessons can be a great advantage for students with speech and language challenges. When a child shows interest and passion for an activity, it creates the ability to develop aptitude in other relating skills.

- **Allergies/Asthma** impact many singers (young and old) who suffer from airborne and seasonal allergies. Be aware that if you are teaching from a home studio, you might have pets, strong smells, plants, or other irritants that can trigger a student's sensitivity. Many allergies can trigger adverse reactions and inhibit the ability to sing and concentrate. Many young allergy sufferers come to their lesson each week with different sinus issues. Helping the child understand the basics of vocal self-care will be useful. Likewise, with asthma triggers, many young children have respiratory issues that can cause difficulties for singing.

- **Dyslexia** can cause a child to struggle with language and musical skills. Recognizing sounds and matching letter and note symbols can be a challenge. Rote learning their music will be beneficial to the the dyslexic singer as it encourages auditory learning as compared to visual learning.

- **Autism Spectrum Disorder** is typically displayed in autistic students who have difficulties with social interactions, communication, and repetitive behaviors. There are varying degrees of the spectrum, and autism can present very differently from child to child. Gaining insight and organizing lesson structure will help the teacher create a safe lesson and learning space for children with these unique attributes. It is common for people with autism to show giftedness in musical aptitude, and integrating them into the private studio can be a benefit to their growth and coping skills. If a teacher does not feel qualified to work with a child experiencing any of these symptoms, it is advised to seek out another teacher or a music therapist who might be a better fit for the student's musical development.

In my own experience, I have witnessed a variety of these attributes over the years. Children mature in many ways. Sometimes it is worth observing and keeping a watchful eye on the progression of behaviors. I have noticed many children outgrow allergies and behavioral conditions with patience. It is never worth mentioning unless it is causing disturbances regularly in the lesson. Recently I had a young nine-year-old student who had a feeling of something stuck in his throat. He would have a limited range on and off from week to week. Since he was only nine years old, it was too early for the onset of puberty, and his overall stature did not suggest a rapid onset of growth. As it became progressively problematic in several songs that were once easy to sing, I mentioned it to the parent. I thought he might have some allergy issues that might need addressing. The parent wasn't sure and paid more attention to his symptoms. Gradually it became worse, and away from singing, he had an episode with significant reflux that landed him in the ER. After seeking medical attention they learned he had severe laryngopharyngeal reflux disease (LPR), and the back of his throat was red and inflamed. In addition, he had extreme irritation in the entire esophagus. The parent was grateful for my observance in the initial recognition of the problem. I handled my remarks carefully from the start of the situation. I never wanted to alarm the parent or the child that something was awry. The last thing a voice teacher wants to do is sound alarms about something negative when all the child wants to focus on is singing fun songs. I recommend the same approach to learning issues. It is not the teacher's job to diagnose a problem. The voice teachers' role is to be aware of the various conditions that can affect the progress in the studio.

> *The information provided here is for the sole purpose of becoming aware of some common physical and mental challenges that children can experience in the voice studio. This is a condensed look at some general conditions and should not be used to attempt any form of diagnosis. If a teacher suspects any issues that are preventing progress in the voice lesson, then the teacher should discuss any concerns carefully and sensitively with the parent.*

Personality

Beyond the information or specific concerns regarding individual circumstances, the teacher should be alert to distinct aspects of children in general. If a voice teacher is new to working with children and has little exposure to the pre-pubescent age group, it might be an adjustment in relating to the specific qualities all children possess. Kids are straightforward and don't hide their emotions. They can be brutally honest, which at times can catch the teacher off guard. Oftentimes the innocence of childhood is filled with ignorant simplicity and can bring tons of free expression to the voice studio. A teacher certainly does not want to subject a child to the scrutiny and demands of adulthood too soon. Allow them to keep creativity and playfulness flowing in their lessons, offering positive reinforcement along the way. When children feel confident in a task, they will have more motivation to keep working. Below are a few examples of some distinctive qualities children bring to the voice studio:

- **Curiosity.** When working with adult singers, the teacher will find that most learners want to know why something is important. Children love to know why, too, but their curiosity is not usually about technical strategies. A child's concern is more about why you have something new on your piano this week. Children are inclined to accept singing technique without questioning a teacher's reasons, especially if offered in a fun manner. Teachers will find that kids are very willing to explore and discover without questioning the motives or feeling embarrassed.

- **Work ethic.** Children are not capable of practicing accurately on their own. They need guidance at home for managing the skills and strategies used in the lesson. Making practice fun and working with a parent will inspire the young singer.

- **Motivation.** Motivation by personal achievement and self-mastery is more common with adults. Children are prone to be motivated by extrinsic rewards like stickers and prizes. Guiding the incentives for children is one of the goals a voice teacher must acquire. Empower the young singers to have autonomy and to set personal victories.

- **Mindset.** Children have a limited amount of prior singing experiences. They have very few preconceived ideas and bring enthusiasm and an open mind to voice lessons. Goal setting is an important task to work on with young children.

- **Sincerity.** Children are emotionally different because they do not hide their feelings and express their moods openly. They love to explore and will enjoy creating and discovering.

Vocal Self-Care

Children are learning how to become self-reliant and independent in many things as they grow and mature. Guiding them in their understanding of how the voice works needs to be geared to their young minds. One aspect to include in the learning process is how to care for their singing voice. Share good vocal health practices with both the parent and the student. Teaching children how to care for their voice should begin at the very start of voice lessons, no matter how old they are. Just like adults, kids need to maintain a healthy lifestyle to keep their growing voice in the best shape as possible. Children are very resilient but still need to be cautious when exposed to a variety of adverse experiences. Some of the basics a child singer can understand and maintain are:

> ### CHILD PROTECTION
> *Voice teachers need to host a child-safe environment that begins with teachers being aware of the ways children and adults interact with each other. Voice teachers need to create a safe place and prevent any wrongful or misunderstood contact with their students. Teachers must be aware of not only their interactions with children, but they need to be alert to any warning signs of abuse that a child might display. Include parents in the lessons with young children, so there is another adult present. Be aware of touching and how it can be confused with the wrong intentions. It is advised to work with children in a "hands-off" approach. Working alone, behind closed doors with a child or children is not recommended.*

- **Hydration.** When studying singing, children need to drink plenty of water and should avoid sugary beverages. They should not be drinking caffeinated beverages regularly and should avoid them on days that they use their singing voices.

- **Allergies.** Closely monitor children who suffer from allergies and be aware of the effects that can appear when singing. Educate and discuss with the parent what preventive measures are being taken at home and make recommendations sensitively and cautiously.

- **Nutrition.** In addition to nurturing their growing bodies with healthy foods, children need to learn about the foods that support healthy singing. Singers of all ages should avoid foods that can cause digestive problems or trigger allergies. Children need to have a nutritious snack before a lesson and performances; they will function much better after they have some caloric intake for energy. Many children are sensitive to foods that contain artificial food dyes, added ingredients, and high-fructose corn syrup. These types of foods can cause behavioral issues and upset stomachs. Various foods affect people differently. Some foods can make a child sleepy, and some can make them hyper. Help them to become aware of how foods affect their performance when singing.

- **GERD and LPR.** Voice teachers must be alert and knowledgeable about the various concerns regarding reflux and how it can affect the voice. Even young children are prone to adverse reactions from gastroesophageal reflux disease (GERD) and laryngopharyngeal reflux disease (LPR). Many children are diagnosed with these conditions and voice teachers should guide students and parents in recognizing the possible symptoms, such as chronic throat clearing and inconsistent huskiness.

- **Medication**. Some children take medications regularly and will need to be watchful of the possible side effects on the voice.

- **Heavy Voice Use**. Teach children to avoid screaming or yelling. Many children are active in sports and need to be aware of how much grunting, cheering and yelling they do on the playing fields. When children are with groups of other children, the intensity level of their voice use becomes much higher. Caution singers against sleepovers and outdoor play before a lesson or performance, to preserve stamina. A teacher should closely monitor a singer with any dysphonia or vocal fatigue. If a teacher hears any lasting raspiness or loss of range (more than a few weeks), the teacher should help locate a pediatric laryngologist and refer the student to get evaluated by a professional.

- **Rest**. Getting enough sleep, especially on the nights before a voice lesson or performance, is important. Sleepy kids in a voice lesson create a challenge for lesson momentum and enjoyment for both the student and the teacher. Children function much better when they are well-rested.

- **Routine**. It will be much easier for children to accomplish tasks and achieve success when they are on a structured daily routine. It is usually Monday lessons and end of summer lessons that have kids off balance because their structured daily routine is out of sync.

With so many facets to health and wellbeing, it's easy to understand how a customized approach must be created based on the individual in order to create a positive, enjoyable experience. Preparing a studio environment for children takes on distinctive qualities. Teachers working with children need to tailor the lessons for young singers with the specific needs and observations that each singer requires.

CHAPTER 4:
Parental Involvement

"An unlimited amount of ability can develop when parent and child are having fun together." —Shinichi Suzuki

Engaging with Parents

In my personal experience as a mother and teacher, I have come to recognize the importance of parental involvement in cultivating good work ethic practices. One of the special opportunities of working with children in the voice studio is the additional chance to involve parents. Adults partnering with their child can create a myriad of beautiful experiences. As we know, there are several unique differences in teaching voice to children, and these beginning singers need to have guidance and discernment from an adult in their learning process. In the studio, the voice teacher should be mentoring not only the child but the parents as well.

Children need parental guidance because they are just beginning to formulate their ideas about the world around them. When parents expose their children to unique experiences, they have a direct result on their child's awareness. A mom, dad, or caregiver should attend the lesson and take notes to guide the experiences from the studio to the home. An adult should be a part of the lessons until the child is of the age at which they can adequately grasp all of the information given in a session by taking notes on their own, recording, and practicing independently. A teacher should not expect a young child to remember the material discussed in each session and think they will go home and practice—by themselves—all the strategies that were shared.

As a teacher, it is important to mentor the parent on how to implement these tasks. Make sure each parent or caregiver takes notes from the start of the lessons. In the early stages, make sure to point out in the instruction when and what the parent should write down. In this way, the parent should be guiding and participating in the practice regimen at home. While teaching the student, the instructor is also showing the parent about the specifics of work ethic, musical literacy, and healthy vocal habits.

Parental involvement will result in better awareness of the child's ability and focus level and provide an opportunity to see how the child works with a teacher. Both students and families will be exposed to a broader range of musical styles and genres. Parents will become in tune with their child and gain incredible insight. As a bonus, parents themselves will grow in their musical and vocal literacy, gaining knowledge, empathy, and understanding.

Dr. Shinichi Suzuki, who established the well-organized and internationally successful *Suzuki Method*, believed that all children develop musical proficiency in the same way they learn their mother tongue. He stated that "talent is no accident at birth" (Suzuki, 1983). The Suzuki music teaching tradition includes "The Suzuki Triangle," a model which consists of active connection between student, parent, and teacher. Voice lessons with young children benefit significantly from this same scenario.

Children are in the hands of their parents. When a young singer shows an interest in singing, it is the parent who pursues voice lessons for their child, acting upon this interest on the child's behalf. For young children under the age of ten, the parent should be an active participant in not only pursuing the lessons but also helping to develop a work ethic. It is especially important for children who are not yet reading fluently on their own. When parents are actively involved, there is a higher chance of success and attainment of skills.

One of my young private students, Eva, came to me when she was just turning five years old. She showed an interest in singing, and her mother had studied voice lessons in college as a non-major. Eva's mother never learned to read music and was excited to enter this journey with her daughter. Eva had two younger siblings at home, one of whom was a newborn. Her mother brought Eva to lessons without her siblings. The lesson time was a unique experience for Eva to have Mom all to herself, where the two of them gained knowledge of musical concepts while bonding through music. Eva continued for many years, and eventually her sisters joined in the fun and started taking lessons too, making it a whole family affair. I love watching family members support one another through the gift of song.

Boundaries

Of course, there are pitfalls to parental involvement, which include the well-intended parent who becomes overly corrective or overly pushy. These behaviors allow another moment of mentoring by the teacher to maintain focus by gently guiding the student to a better place for growth. It is up to the teacher to set boundaries. Make clear to the parent what the expectations are and how to execute them. The teacher needs to be confident and secure in teaching style and strategies. By offering a well-organized and prepared lesson scenario, there is less of a chance for interruptions.

The **overly-corrective parent** interjects every time the child does not react or behave in the manner that the parent approves of and overrides what the teacher is trying to accomplish. This conduct can become very distracting in the lesson for all involved. These unwelcomed interruptions usually result in the child becoming even more inattentive because the child is constantly seeking the parent's approval. If there is ever an occasion that the teacher is not satisfied with the results of parental behavior, the teacher should discuss the interruptions with the parent—outside of the lesson, not in front of the student—or gently make clear the boundaries that are set by re-directing certain behaviors. The participation of the parent in a lesson should be unobtrusive. The child needs to be unaware of his or her presence and become fully engaged in the instruction led by the instructor. The student should be seeking the approval of the teacher and not the parent.

The other pitfall to parental involvement is the **overly-pushy parent**. In this scenario, the parent treats the voice teacher as an employee and makes demands that are not in the child's best interest. Some parents want to see their children succeed at higher standards than the child may be capable of achieving at the moment. Perhaps the parent wants the child to take on an extraordinary feat of performing or work on specific repertoire. In all cases, instructors must stand their ground on protecting the student's growing instrument, while maintaining their own reputation regarding expertise and respect. I am a mother of three; I raised a child actor, a highly competitive violinist, and a ballet dancer. I have experience with stage moms, violin tiger moms, and dance moms of many varieties. I have seen how the behavior of overly pushy parents can manifest, and it never bodes well for the child or the adults involved. If the teacher experiences a pushy parent and it is challenging to mentor them, use an approach that fosters a place where healthy and beautiful singing is an area of growth for the child, and the teacher's opinion is respected.

Establish boundaries and create a thriving learning environment with parents by implementing these strategies:

- The parent should be only an active listener during lessons, preparing to be a guide and mentor for home practice.

- Teach the parents how to take notes.

- Recommend ways to practice and reinforce the skills at home.

- Offer suggestions on how they can incorporate more musical experiences into their family life (see live concerts or musical performances regularly to expose their children to performers of all ages).

- Advise parents on the many ways they can offer a variety of music genres into the listening choices at home and in the car.

- Help parents see the many benefits of their musical experience and how they can adopt many of the skills into other areas of the child's development (speech skills, reading, and comprehension, motor learning skills, etc.).

SECTION II
Vocal Technique for the Child Singer

CHAPTER 5:
Using Structure to Teach Self-Mastery

Talent is an ongoing journey and not a final destination.

How do we teach self-mastery to children? I was recently attending a gathering of voice teachers who were passionate about working with children in the private studio. We were sharing stories and collaborating about the fun games we use in our lessons to keep kids engaged. One of the voice teachers asked about the ways we can incorporate vocal technique into the lessons, and several of the teachers declared that they don't teach technical execution to children; they keep the focus on fun musical games and activities that encourage an open mindset about a love for music and singing. Others went on to say that getting into technical procedures with children was not a good idea that technique was too stuffy and boring a topic for children to grasp.

I was taken by surprise when so many teachers spoke out against teaching prepubescent singers anything technical. My personal belief is that children can and should learn formative technique, and the earlier the better. As previously discussed, some people have the idea that children studying vocal technique is harmful for the growing voice. With that logic, if a child can incur damage in singing lessons, then they can also hurt their voices if they sing without any guidance. If a child suffers some voice trauma from singing, it is most likely an association of misuse and over-use. In this case, a child can develop a voice disorder from repeated injury. An observant and knowledgeable voice teacher does not allow this to happen.

One cause of repeated trauma from unguided singing is from using unhealthy forms of phonation. Some children imitate sounds they hear, which can result in vocal issues if they don't understand limitations and the feeling of healthy vocal sounds. If voice teachers show their young students how to care for their voice and how to be aware of the intensity and duration guidelines, then we can teach young singers technical strategies without fear of hurting or causing damage. The focus with young children is to keep all types of singing within limits regarding intensity and duration, which means, that the child should not be singing for long periods and should not be singing too intensely with forced and loud singing. Efficient singing is the goal, and this can be achieved by learning technical strategies with an experienced voice teacher, who understands the unique attributes and needs of the child singer.

The Reasons for Vocal Technique for Children

This ideology of "no technique" for children must change. Of course we can teach vocal techniques to children! However, first, we must outline what "technique" actually means and why voice teachers believe that children should steer clear of this notion. Children are capable of understanding technical concepts when explained in a way that makes sense to them. We see this model in ballet classes for children in the pre-school years. They don't simply twirl about for 45 minutes; they are learning how to use the body technically while engaging in a way that feels fun.

As a Suzuki violin parent, I watched firsthand as my children learned the fundamental elements of violin technique even at the tender age of three. The very first thing a violin student learns is how to hold the violin and carry it from place to place under their arm. Then they learn how to stand in a position with their feet firmly situated. Next, they set the violin on their shoulder. After the child learns these formative steps, they are ready to make a sound on the instrument. The teacher then begins instruction on the many technical skills required to make a beautiful tone on their fiddle. The young child quickly and systematically builds on a foundation of learning skills that need sophistication and technical savvy. They learn mastery of skills on an instrument even before they start preschool. Everything that we do as teachers in a lesson should be about technique, and for children, yes, it should be fun. It doesn't have to be one or the other.

The Master-Apprentice model has contributed to the way many voice teachers execute technique. For many years vocal pedagogy has been taught around "classical" voice training, which emphasizes a certain style of acoustics and resonance. "Classical" is not the type of technical training a young singer needs. Children require a foundation in good singing habits. By comparison, a young ballerina who starts dancing at age five is not ready for the challenges of going *en pointe*. The young dancer must develop strength in the legs, ankles, and back before there are demands of more sophisticated dancing. This same idea can also be prevalent with children in sports. A young boy is not ready to throw a curveball. His body is still developing, and there is a risk of elbow and shoulder injury.

In dance and sports, children are welcome to participate at early ages. They learn the basics of technical proficiency that guide them along the path of self-mastery. Children who start young have a smoother transition into the more sophisticated execution of skills as they mature developing kinesthetic awareness and aptitude. They don't have to wait until their muscular system is in place before they can enjoy these activities. Children want to play sports, take dance classes, and sing. Just because we are not learning advanced techniques at an earlier age doesn't mean a child is not learning technical proficiency. The elemental things we teach young singers are a foundation for formalizing the more advanced techniques. While developing early technical skills, young singers are establishing basic musical concepts in a fun and nurturing environment.

Benefits of Mastering Musical Concepts

When children learn to master musical concepts, they gain many benefits to their overall emotional and educational development. Teaching musical and vocal techniques can be rewarding and far-reaching. In addition to learning the basics of singing technique, children are developing many other life skills.

Some of the many benefits that can improve when children take singing lessons:

- Public speaking, confidence, and poise
- Speech and language development
- Self-discipline and self-awareness
- Memorization skills

- Language and reading proficiency

- Music reading proficiency

- Work ethic

- Growth mindset

- Cultivating a strong foundation for vocal development

Teaching children technical proficiency, however, requires an organized lesson structure. When beginning a new student, the teacher needs to evaluate where the student is developmentally and what technical skills they already possess. A plan must be devised to help the student grow based on the initial assessment. Similar to a doctor, the voice teacher must assess by making a plan of action for growth.

Evaluating the Individual Singer

In foundational work with children, the teacher must know what to address and how to execute the technical points with each singer. Start by evaluating the singer on a fundamental basis and periodically throughout your work with them. (See "New Student Observation and Follow-Up Form" in the Appendix, p. 117). Keep notes on weekly progress, and check in with the previous conclusions for re-evaluation. Some of the main points for evaluations are:

- **Demeanor**. Does the child appear focused, unfocused, sassy, bored, moody, or shy? How is the child's overall poise and temperament?

- **Parents**. What is the overall relationship like between parent and child? Is the child dependent on the parent or always prompted by the parent? Is the parent pushy or overly corrective with the child? Also observe the parent's voice quality, as it will serve as an indicator of what the child models at home.

- **Body awareness**. Notice how the child stands when preparing to sing. Is the body relaxed, floppy, tense, exaggerated, or shoulders too high?

- **Musical ability**. Does the child play any instruments or read music yet? Does the child have a good ear for repeating sung pitches in tune?

- **Overall singing voice quality**. Observe if any sounds and distinctions appear raspy, breathy, or quiet. Notice if there are inefficiencies with forced, pushed, or constricted sounds.

- **Speaking voice quality.** Take note of any characteristics in the student's speaking voice. Does the child speak softly, or is there any huskiness to their sound?

- **Diction and articulation**. How are the overall speech sounds? Are there any noticeable speech delays or letter sounds that the child can't pronounce accurately?

- **Vocal range**. During vocalization exercises, take note of how high and low the child can sing to identify their vocal range. Also observe how they use the different registers when ascending and descending.

- **Registration.** Discovering the different qualities of sound each singer can produce with ease (head voice and chest voice) and how they balance these functions. Are there any breaks and dramatic changes from one quality to the other?

- **Expression**. Notice if the student is animated when they speak and when they sing. Are they the same or different when speaking and singing?

Use these key points to gain a general idea of what to focus on with each young singer. Once the teacher has determined the skill level and has devised the plan of action, it is time to work into a structured lesson curriculum. Offering a systematic course of study allows the teacher and student instructional objectives that are organized and strategic.

In the following chapters, a five-step system for lesson structuring will guide the teacher in understanding how to organize content that corresponds to the objectives for overall growth and development. This outline is designed to guide the teacher through a series of technical strategies aimed at young children and their success in mastering foundational singing techniques.

CHAPTER 6:
The Born 2 Sing Kids Five-Step System: Achieving Technical Success with Children

"Every child is talented. Any child who is properly trained can develop musical ability, just as all children develop the ability to speak their mother tongue. The potential of every child is unlimited."

—*Shinichi Suzuki*

Lesson structuring and pacing are essential ingredients for achieving technical success and mastery of skills with children. The structure of lesson time can be a problem when a teacher is new to working with young kids. When I first started taking voice lessons, after begging my mom for what seemed like years, I was 13 years old. I remember my first teacher, Jill Goodsell. Her studio was in the dining room of her home. I thought it was magical that there was a grand piano, surrounded by bookcases filled with musical scores, in the place of a dining table and a china cabinet. I had a 30-minute lessons with Ms. Goodsell which began with a 15-minute warm-up that included Lütgen exercises. We would then spend the next 15 minutes singing my repertoire. I sang mostly Golden Age musical theatre songs and selections from *24 Italian Art Songs and Arias*. I remember buying a small tape recorder and a package of cassette tapes, and I recorded each lesson on them.

I experienced nearly this same scenario for the duration of my singing career. Of course I advanced in skills, repertoire, and technology, but while these shifted and the length of the lesson increased, the basic format remained the same: vocalize, then repertoire. These two areas still comprise most voice lessons for teen and adult singers. It works well for them, but this format is not the best approach for children in the voice studio.

When working with young singers in the private studio, a teacher should cover other areas of musical and singing proficiency. Children need more concentration on a variety of skills, and their attention spans are short, requiring a variety of strategies. Pacing the lesson traditionally—vocalizing, then repertoire—does not offer a comprehensive learning environment. Offering an array of activities is most suitable and all-encompassing. A voice lesson experience for young children needs a new and unique formula for success. If a teacher is new to teaching pre-pubescent voices, the first thing to prepare is an outline based on the initial evaluation. I designed the *Born 2 Sing Kids Five-Step System* to achieve the goal of efficient lesson pacing. These five steps include attention around:

- Mind-body awareness
- Breath and posture
- Musicianship training
- Vocalization practice
- Repertoire building

Children need a lesson curriculum designed to meet their needs for fundamental vocal and musical growth. Included in this curriculum is the ability to adapt and change with each child.

Structuring the Lesson

When pacing a lesson with solid content and instructional objectives, a 45-minute lesson goes by very quickly. The teacher can engage the child in fun activities designed to build the skills required for efficient and inspired singing. In my experience, students are rarely ready to leave when a lesson is over. They are in a happy mood and say things like, "Is it time to go already?" Each segment should last about 5-10 minutes, moving onto another task smoothly and sequentially. The flow helps the child stay engaged and interested, without an overly long stretch on a specific topic. At the same time, the young voice is not over-working the intensity or duration of vocal use. These small segments make it easy for the child to engage and learn.

There are many benefits to working in small segments. The young singer can explore an array of vocal and musical skills. All of these skills work to collectively make the youngster a better singer, musician, and person. The focus should be on readiness and aptitude in each lesson. In this five-step system the voice teacher is not merely "coaching" the student on songs, but rather "teaching" the child how to sing healthily and artfully. Children can work on skills including sight-singing, articulating constants, and projecting their voices, without overdoing these activities.

An additional benefit to using the five-step system is the ability to pace the voice lesson to fit the needs of each student or groups of students. I regularly teach small and large group singing classes using the same process. When there are a variety of tasks and skills to work on, it is easy to integrate them for a variety of learning environments. Earlier I shared my previous experience teaching general music in elementary schools. It was there that I first created this system, as I had to quickly formulate a curriculum and discern the aptitude levels in each grade. It was from these formative classroom years I realized children enjoy singing and can learn singing technique in private lessons, small and large group classes.

Another good reason to keep things organized and planned out is that each weekly session brings a new phase with the student. Kids are continually changing in maturity and behaviors. A child that was rowdy last week might be exhausted and crabby the next week. Sometimes a teacher will adapt and skip one area of focus to get onto the next task. Other times, the teacher will find the student is enjoying a particular exercise and is about to embark on a new awareness, so they spend extra time on an activity. It is the teacher's job to have a set plan of action ready to go with a mixture of options in case they may need to redirect.

Before diving into the curriculum, it is important to evaluate where each singer is in their level of singing aptitude. The teacher should make sure that the objective of each student's progress always has intention. Find time to write down and observe the progression of each student. The instructor should have goals for what they want to achieve with each singer. Since the teacher and student are working in a private setting, there should not be a strict timeline on advancement. Meet the student where they are from week to week in their progress. Some goals for young singers are not exclusive to music and singing proficiency but may include: developing emotional intelligence through art and empathy, practicing growth mindset skills, cultivating self-confidence, self-esteem, and self-love for their unique voice. As a private teacher, it will be gratifying to nurture the child's growing mind and voice.

Kids Will Be Kids

Remember that children communicate in an honest, direct, and straightforward manner. Kids will tell you what they are genuinely thinking and mean it most sincerely. Sometimes this can be uncomfortable, and other times, it is refreshing and eye-opening. Young kids may often comment on the teacher's appearance from hairstyles to clothing choices. Children hold nothing back and tell you what they think. Their curiosity, innocence, and obedience, however, make them the ideal voice student.

It is for all these reasons that following the Five-Step System will offer a teacher the ability to have tremendous success when working with children. These young singers are unique and require a different set of teaching strategies. While teaching children is not something that everyone enjoys, it can be a wondrous and inspiring experience. Let's explore each of the five steps.

CHAPTER 7:
The Five-Step System:
Step One – Mind and Body Warm-Ups

Mind...Set...Go!

Have you ever had a student arrive at a lesson and not appear to be ready to work? Maybe something occurred at home or school that has caused emotional distress, or perhaps they feel physically debilitated in some way. A teacher can wonder how to start a lesson when the student is not in the state of readiness to begin focusing. Keeping in mind the goals for that student's lesson, the objective for every student should be to start with a proper mindset.

My student Martin, who has a refreshing intellectual curiosity, comes to his lesson with a little bit of nervous energy and constantly strokes his fingers through his hair. He is aware of his nervous habits, but in the moment, it can be challenging for him to redirect that energy. After watching one of his performance videos, he added "stop fidgeting" to his list of goals.

Occasionally, I like to begin Martin's lessons with meditation. I have him lie down on a yoga mat and practice stillness. Once he can get reasonably comfortable, I ask him to close his eyes and bring his awareness inward. We practice stillness and breathing. With his hands on his belly, I ask him to pant like a dog. When he feels how his stomach moves, it helps bring awareness to his body, mind, and breathing mechanism. Instead of doing standing exercises to stretch and warm up the body, Martin often needs to warm up his mind and his breath. He needs to become more aware of how singing is a very internal skill. Most of the work we do as singers relates to feeling sensations, and the changes we often need to make are nuances and subtle shifts. Martin understands many of the concepts, but needs to learn how to focus inward.

Step One

Step One in a voice lesson is starting with mind and body. Some kids are naturally more focused than others, but all of them want to wiggle and have fun. Start with energetic movement exercises that awaken the body, or, like Martin, begin with gentle activities that bring internal awareness by encouraging imagination and concentration. Working on the body and mind helps get the student in a state of readiness. It also helps the child focus on the teacher and not the parent observing the lesson. Use these exercises to target one-on-one collaboration with the student. Every week each student will require different strategies.

Singing in front of someone for the first time can make anyone a little nervous. For kids, this comes out in obvious behavioral issues. I have had kids come into their first few lessons and hide behind their mom. Once I had a mom arrive at the door for a lesson with no child. The mom told me her child had fallen asleep on the drive. Mom set her stuff down in the studio and went back to the car to retrieve the student. *"Great, now what?"* I thought. A sleeping child wasn't what I had planned for our first full lesson. This is when quick thinking is necessary, and this is a skill you'll need to sharpen when working with children. I rolled out a yoga mat and enlisted help from several stuffed animals. I coaxed the singer from her mother's lap to join me, with the toys on the yoga mat. We slowly and gently stretched our bodies and sang the "Wiggle Song." After the singer was alert and ready to explore, we did some fun echo songs. After several minutes of waking up our bodies, minds, and singing voices, we continued the lesson with focus and direction.

With mind and body exercises, a teacher must first get a young singer excited about the voice lesson and to draw their attention to the teacher, diverting their thoughts away from the parent or any other distractions in the room. The first technique a child is learning is how to focus. Such consideration helps to set the grounds for the lesson and to guide the overall experience with concentration. Exercise the mind and body simultaneously. Get the child to pay attention and follow directions, while having fun learning necessary singing skills at the same time. These kinds of exercises can also address relaxation techniques, posture, and alignment. Including musical games—like marching to a steady beat—is also very useful and fun.

Some of my favorite kinesthetic warm-ups to do with young singers are stretches, yoga postures, call and response games, echo songs, and rhythmic coordination games—anything that encourages the body to move. Movement is a great way to get a child to shake their "sillies" out. Lead the way, but as you go along, anticipate what it is that the student needs today in their lesson.

Using Props

Props can be a great way of helping to focus, as well as with explaining concepts and encouraging movement. Props can be helpful for fidgeting hands and nervous energy, for follow-through in movement, and for allowing singers to demonstrate their thoughts about a concept without having to come up with the right words. Some singers create lots of tension in their shoulders when they breathe. Incorporate specific stretches or movements, that bring awareness to this area. It is essential to explain to young singers that while we don't want rigid tension in our bodies when we sing, we also do not want to be a wiggly limp noodle. How we use our muscles for singing require what I refer to as "tonus." One of my vocal pedagogy professors, John Paul White, used this description, and I find even little kids can understand this concept. I explain that "tonus" is like having a little bit of stiffness without being overly rigid. I let my singers demonstrate what they think the differences might look like by using an example with their own body or a prop like a stretchy noodle or resistance band. Anything that can aid the child's understanding can be useful and fun. We want the muscles to be ready to respond with active participation.

Copy-Cat Games

Copy-cat games are also excellent for establishing focus, whether it is a song, solfege pattern, or rhythmic sequence. I give my kids a short phrase and have them repeat it back to me. They love the "copy-cat" game, and it engages them while focusing attention on the teacher. The benefit is when I make the focus on a particular skill that I know the singer needs, they are practicing that technique, and they don't even know it. I have a student currently who has a hard time accessing his head voice register. When I introduce copy-cat activities at the beginning of the lesson, I often choose one that requires a light head voice sound. Introducing concepts in a clever way is useful for those young singers who are reluctant to explore a specific skill, like head voice singing. Introducing new and different sounds is always easier through imaginative play. While focusing on a specific drill during the mind and body warm-ups, the teacher is already introducing technical strategies for singing. Interweaving these actions is a clever approach for hesitant children. Just as a parent gets their child to eat vegetables by cutting them into fun shapes or hiding them in a tasty sauce, we can disguise vocal technique—in each of the five steps—in the most delightful way!

Men using a copy-cat approach in encouraging head voice singing may already know that if the male sings in his normal range, the child cannot necessarily abstractly understand that he or she is to sing an octave higher. This is particularly true for boys. A male teacher may need to sing in a falsetto range, in the octave where the child sings, for a child to understand which pitch to imitate.

Taking Notes

For the parents attending the lesson, observing these activities and taking notes is essential. They should be encouraged to lead the practice sessions at home. Parents can record videos or voice memos of the lessons, which aid in at-home practice routines. Besides helping their child to make progress with singing, it is a beautiful experience for parents to be able to watch their child create art and build a skill set that elevates their knowledge in abilities, even far beyond the singing itself.

Remember that every mind and body warm-up exercise should have an intentional objective. The voice teacher should take notes on the progress of each lesson to make sure that growth continues to build from week to week. Each skill should be age-appropriate and developmentally useful. While it can be fun to play games in a lesson and encourage movement with the mind-body warm-ups, make sure that each task can relate to the goals you have in mind for that student. Being armed with many tools and ready to tackle unexpected turns is essential for having success with the child singer.

If you are not sure where to begin with choosing these exercises, Section III of this book will provide you with specific activities for the various ages and steps for lesson structure.

CHAPTER 8:
The Five-Step System:
Step Two – Breathing and Posture

Breath is the bedrock for vocal sound.

After warming up the mind and body, the young singer is ready to work more attentively on comprehensive singing skills. Some of the technical groundwork for singing requires a rooted knowledge of respiratory mechanics, and guiding youngsters in breathing techniques can be a little tricky. Kids can often overcomplicate things by exaggerating. Just ask a child to take a deep breath. The action often results in artificial responses with a big heave of the shoulders and lifting of the rib cage. Gently guiding a young singer to a basic understanding of how they should breathe for phonation is the goal.

There are many beneficial reasons for working on breath strategies for children. Not only is connecting with your breath a therapeutic and relaxing practice, but it also helps children learn the "ground-up" concept of how the voice works.

Breath Motion

The first thing a young singer should learn is about breath motion. Child singers should be aware of ways the breath comes into the body and how the breath goes out of the body, achieving this motion without over-exaggeration. As a child builds on the understanding of breath flow without tension, they can begin to develop an understanding of breath stability. Once a child reaches the tween years, they have more muscle coordination and brain function and are ready to build breath management in regards to breath stamina and vocal phrasing.

With any aged singer, voice instructors work on a relaxed inhalation without creating tension in the neck or shoulders. While it is possible for some, do not expect young children to be masters of breath management and long phrases anytime soon; the goal is to bring awareness to the function. The pre-pubescent body is still growing, and children do not have the full lung capacity for increased duration of breath flow.

Once they learn the basics of gently moving air in and out of the body, young singers must learn about stability, without force, on the expiration. Most young children have the natural instinct to blast the air out quickly. Stabilizing tone and breath is unquestionably a critical aspect of singing technique. As singers develop, they will learn to draw attention to the core muscles of the abdomen, lower back, hips, and pelvis, to enhance their vocal sound with energy, and steadiness. Enlightening a young singer on the proper ways to inhale and exhale is the essence of good technique. Voice teachers need to teach kid-friendly exercises in language that children can understand. Using props and fun techniques will be discussed using the various ages and stages later in the curriculum breakdown.

A child can understand at an early age that breath for singing is different from breathing for everyday life. As explained in *The Diagnosis and Correction of Vocal Faults* (McKinney, 2005, p. 48), there are differences in breathing for existence and breathing for singing. When a singer breathes for vocal sound, there is a four-stage process: inhalation, suspension, phonation, and recovery. Breathing for existence only uses three of these stages and the rate in which the breath moves can be much slower. When humans naturally breathe through typical stage, the intake is slower than the exhalation. When a singer breathes for the vocal sound, the inhalation is generally swift, and the expiration occurs during the prolonged period of phonation.

The Journey of Sound

As a voice teacher, it is important to inspire young singers by sharing some kid-friendly concepts regarding how the voice works. Define the parts that make up vocal sound in simple terms. All instruments have three parts: a generator, a vibrator, and a resonator. For young singers, these three parts can be described as having a starting place in the lungs, a sound maker in the throat, and an amplifier in the mouth.

The stages of making vocal sound can also be described to children in a set of three steps: preparation, launching, and traveling. Vocal sound makes a journey through our bodies. Just like taking a boat ride, the first stage is the preparation or send-off, then launching from the dock, and then the journey continues on the buoyancy of the water. Our singing sound makes this journey; the motion of air launches the sound through the vocal folds and then travels through the mouth to create buoyancy of tone. Throughout the entire journey, there is stability where the breath maintains the motion. Just like the boat ride, we don't want to sink. Air moves through our bodies, and through our mouth, which creates new and exciting sounds for what I like to call "The Journey of Sound."

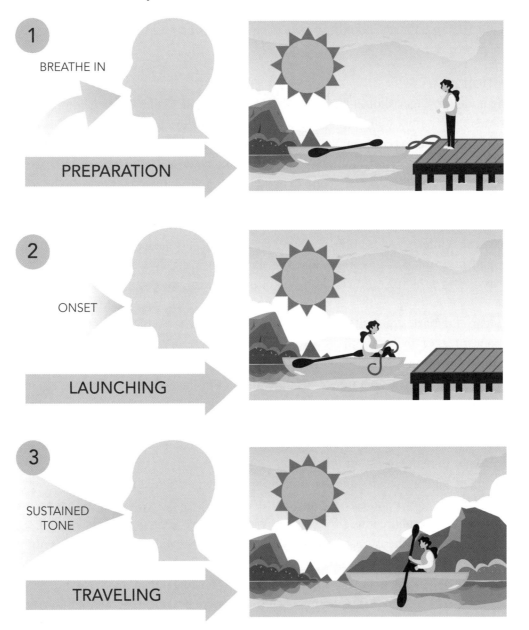

Starting with the "preparation" image helps youngsters to connect to the idea that their breath carries them on a journey. This idea helps to lay a basic foundation in creating an elemental readiness that includes consideration to body awareness. Young singers will develop an understanding of the workings of their body when they take in and expel their breath.

Posture

Body awareness and posture alignment are elemental in breathing techniques. Instruction on the ways to keep the body relaxed and the shoulders staying away from their ears is necessary for proper function. Young singers must develop skills that bring awareness to expansion in and around the torso area. Engaging those "core" muscles, a child must learn that breath is not efficient when they gasp, heave their shoulders, or create tension and tightness that is overly exaggerated. To secure this understanding of good posture, begin by standing alongside the student and activate body-lengthening stretches. Reaching and pretending to climb by extending arms up overhead are not only fun physical activities, but create movement that instills good posture, which is required for an efficient breathing technique.

How a singer stands to sing is as important as how they take in the breath. It is very important to help the child make a connection that these two skills work together. Posture exercises can be achieved standing and lying down. When on the floor, guide the student to feel how their back makes contact with the ground. They should be able to sense the straight, not rigid, lengthening of the body. When the student stands up, help them to create this same sense of lengthening and straight posture—reminding them about tonus and how our bodies should be strong and firm but not stiff and rigid. Asking a child to stand tall will often result in another over-exaggeration. Sometimes young kids think that standing tall requires standing at attention like a soldier. Help them to feel that "tonus" perception. Tall, not rigid and firm, not floppy.

Address beginning breathing strategies on the floor in a horizontal position. When students are lying on their backs, have them place a small stuffed animal or toy on their stomach. When they breathe in, they should notice the lifting motion, which can be described as a lift-off. When they exhale, the toy should lower back down to the landing place. To create playful animation, pretend the toy is making a journey on the breath. Teaching about expansion on the inhale will require patience and repetition with young singers. The natural tendency is to pull in their belly on an inhalation. Persistence, empathy, and determination by the teacher will help overcome this challenge. Children need lots of repetition.

To help students with busy/nervous energy like my student Martin, I often start in the horizontal phase to feel grounded mentally and get connected with the breath right away. The mind-body warm-ups can naturally progress into breathing exercises. Breathing for singing can be included as an extension to the first stage of the lesson. Each lesson and each student require attention to different skill sets.

Mindful Breathing

As mentioned, some of the pitfalls that young singers create are related to over-exaggeration. Many beginning students throughout the lifespan tend to draw in too much breath, too fast. This impulse creates a tightening of the muscular system. Inspiration should happen with freedom and openness. Slowing down the intake at first will help foster the correct muscular response. Narrowing the passageway with the lips or straw can help approximate the breath intake and direct the child to imagine drinking in the air. Ask them to pretend as though they are drinking a tasty smoothie or their favorite beverage. Children love anything imaginative and asking them to sip in the air and savor its deliciousness will help them slow down. Always look for fun and engaging ways to guide the formative understanding for children singers. Using mental images and imagination fosters creativity.

Note: Working with children does not mean that you should deprive children of fact-based teaching. Using imagery is not intended to take away from the science behind singing, but to help keep the understanding of the mechanism fun and inspiring for kids. When talking about mindful breathing, it is crucial that the voice teacher avoid using non-factual phrases like "sing/support from the diaphragm" for the sake of keeping it simple and employing imagery so that kids can understand. While it is true that sound is supported by maintaining a stability of airflow, the diaphragm is not an active participant in the experience of expelling air while phonating in any way, and children should not be led to technical misconceptions that will lead to a disruption in growth and understanding later down the line.

When addressing posture and breath mechanics with children it is important to guide the student to a place where they can understand the basics of how their body functions when singing in simple terms they can understand. In these first two steps with students, we establish the foundational concepts of mindset, body awareness, focus, respiration, and posture. Embracing these concepts at an early age can lay a good foundation for not only a productive voice lesson, but efficient singing for years to come.

CHAPTER 9:
The Five-Step System: Step Three – Musicianship

"How do you know a soprano is at the door? She can't find her key, and she doesn't know when to come in."

I've heard jokes about singers like this since I was in college, and admittedly many of them strike a chord of humor. But casual remarks of singers not being "musicians" ring throughout many a music school hall, and that belief has somehow permeated the general public. Recently, I was at the doctor's office, and the nurse asked me what I do. I told her I was a professional singer and voice teacher. She then asked me if I was also a musician and if I played any instruments. I was a little perplexed by that question, because of course I am a musician. I don't have to play an instrument to be qualified as a musician; a musician is anyone who plays or performs music. So why is it that singers are often not classified as musicians?

Most voice teachers don't devote enough time to teaching music theory and ear training in lessons. As we now know, the master-apprentice model has affected the content of voice lesson methodology. The average voice lesson in the traditional sense only focuses on vocalization and repertoire. That leaves singers to work on musicianship outside of the voice lesson. If voice teachers transmit more practical methods in musicianship training early on, students will cultivate the skills on how to read and hear music, without needing to be steered to piano lessons as a pre-requisite to singing. Laying a strong foundation in these concepts can establish our singers as well-rounded musicians. Children can learn to read music at the same time they are learning to read words.

Becoming a Singing Musician

The third step in the Five-Step System concerns comprehensive musicianship skills. Most vocal artists begin singing by rote learning. They establish their technique by imitation and not reading the notes. Learning music by ear is natural and also related to the mother-tongue approach. If a singer can learn to read music and not just learn by ear, they have a much better chance of developing their unique sound and ability. In this way, the artist compliments their unparalleled quality by not merely copying someone else. Some of the best singers not only have beautiful tone and expression, but are also considered significant musicians by their ability to hear, read, and reproduce pitches with ease. They can learn a piece of music by sight-reading and not just by ear. One of the many arguments against teaching singing at an early age is that many well-intentioned music educators believe that young children should begin formal music education by studying piano or a stringed instrument, since these instruments are well proven to develop the musical ear and note-reading abilities. There is no doubt that by college age, pianists are among the most well-trained overall musicians. Their ability to hear harmonic progressions and read 4-part music in bass and treble clefs is among many of their talents.

Pianists' exceptional musicianship is often the result of the countless years they spend playing two or more parts, and the years of focus they have spent on cultivating theory and ear training proficiency. Violinists and other string players also have an advantage; much of their training and concentration is spent getting every note in tune. Many instrumentalists spend quality lesson time with instruction devoted to theory and note reading. Rarely do highly skilled classical pianists or string players learn solely by ear.

Perhaps singers are not viewed as musicians because, traditionally, they do not spend adequate time in lessons learning and ripening their reading and listening skills. Adding time in each lesson to formulate and teach the basis for musicianship is a must in every voice lesson for every age.

Resources

Is it crucial to find the right resources and develop a course of action. For the child singer, it is essential to begin a building block of skills, one step at a time. I use the Full Voice workbook series by Nikki Loney and Mim Adams in my studio. These books are helpful and brilliant in teaching a sequential and comprehensive theory and ear training system to young singers. They utilize the tonic sol-fa structure, which is based around "moveable do" and which came out of the early music solfege system. The Full Voice books integrate the hand signs developed in nineteenth-century England by the Reverend John Curwen.

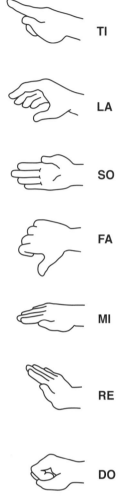

Curwen designed the hand signs as a way of teaching singing techniques in Sunday school programs. He discovered that this technique was beneficial for singers of all ages in learning how to sight-read music. Using a frame of reference that incorporates the solfege system is very helpful in the voice lesson for young singers to have an awareness of aural skills, pitch, and sight-reading abilities. Adding kinesthetic movements in the body helps young students connect with the sound. The action of sound production occurs internally in a singer and is not something that can be seen or touched, as it is for instrumentalists—so having a tactical way to associate pitches as they relate to one another can be very useful for many singers. The Full Voice books also teach basic note reading and musical notation. A bonus in the books is the assessments on performance practices for singers. My young students enjoy their musicianship workbooks, which provide fun exercises to practice in the studio and for reinforcement at home. The student and parent can readily see the progress they are making, which can be a challenge in voice lessons when the progression of mastery is not visual and easy to measure.

Fundamental Skills

If a teacher chooses not to use a system or series of workbooks with their students, it is helpful to understand some guidelines when incorporating musical concepts in a singing lesson. Listed here are the skills I believe should be reinforced by all beginning singers of any age:

- How to keep a steady beat
- Understand basics regarding tempo, form, dynamics, harmony, meter, melody, and tone color
- Learn history of music and how it relates to culture, style, and composers

Adding little lessons and moments of enrichment in these areas helps to create a well-rounded and artistic singer. It also encourages better citizenship to learn a variety of skills and knowledge.

First and foremost, a singer should develop competency in matching pitch. Some singers, young and old, have natural ability for hearing and matching the correct notes, while other students can match pitch, but only in certain parts of their range (we will discuss this further in the chapter regarding vocalization exercises). Still others have to work harder to grasp this proficiency. Practicing a solfege system using tonic sol-fa, or numbers, helps singers develop a tactile means for pitch matching and other aspects of aural skills. According to a recent interview with Nikki Loney, creator of The Full Voice Music Inc., "Solfege is an invaluable system that allows students to sing without accompaniment and develop independent singing skills. Young singers do not have the security of an instrument to hide behind. Solfege offers a visual tool for singers who are just learning musical concepts like tones, semitones, scales, and triads" (N. Loney, personal communication, September 6, 2019).

When teaching theory and ear training, it is inspiring for the student to keep it fun. Creating games and musical activities will keep it engaging. As Loney says, "When singers are having fun they smile, breathe deeper, sing better and they retain far more information."

Like all aspects of the Five-Step System, each step can be integrated into other phases of the learning session. For example, when working on mind and body focus, use a copycat solfege pattern. The teacher can sign and sing a three or four-note tonic sol-fa pattern (usually stepwise, especially for the beginner) and ask the singer to repeat it back. Using the same concept, perform a rhythmic pattern as a copycat game. Kids will find this particularly fun, and in the group classes, they can get very engaged and competitive with one another, which inspires a growth mindset.

All students learn at different paces and come to lessons with varying degrees of musical ability. A young child aged 5-7, or a beginning student in the discovery stage of singing, should be learning how to keep a steady beat, match pitch, and identify ascending and descending melodic patterns. Introducing simple musical symbols at this age is also fundamental. When children are young and just starting their singing lessons, rote learning their songs will be the first stage. As they begin to gain note reading proficiency, they can begin to integrate those skills gradually. Invite the student to use the score as a discovery page by locating symbols and concepts that they are learning in theory. In this way, the student will begin to identify what they are singing and reading.

Around the time children are entering the third grade, ages 8-9, they are becoming fluent in their reading skills at school. Young singers at these ages are ready to begin reading their music notation exclusively from the musical score. Still encouraging listening skills, the singer should start reading music more consistently. By the time a child is reading their spoken language fluently and better able to grasp the concepts of musical notation, they are ready to read the musical score when learning a new song. Children in this age category should be able to know more complex musical terminology, including note and rest values, tempo, and dynamics. This same development applies to an older student who is new to music and singing lessons. Preparing vocalists to read music and hear what is in the score is the ultimate goal.

Correlating a variety of skills is helpful to their overall understanding of musical proficiency. Recently, Tessa, one of my students in the third grade, was experiencing challenges with motivation and grasping some of the musical concepts in her theory workbook. I knew from a previous conversation that Tessa had started learning the recorder in her music class at school. I invited her to bring the recorder to her voice lesson. She was having some struggles grasping the techniques required for getting a pleasant tone and learning her first song on the recorder. Together, we quickly discovered the many benefits this skill could add to her singing expertise. Tessa was working on the song "Hot Cross Buns," a simple melody of only three notes. We broke down the elements into small little segments. Learning to develop the right amount of breath pressure required to produce a good tone on the recorder, and the tricky skills of covering the holes to get the desired note, was a great learning comparison for how we produce vocal sound. The theory aspect provided even more advantages. "Hot Cross Buns" starts with a three-note, descending pattern, on mi-re-do. This lesson helped her to put her mind, breath, and fingers to work, connecting all the dots. Tessa discovered how she could sing the same pattern with solfege symbols, lyrics, or even sing the fingering for the recorder. We had fun integrating these skills to make the connection of how so many musical concepts can build off of one another. This correlation to singing regarding breath stability, note reading, and technique was a real triumph for her.

Voice teachers need to empower their young singers in the advancement of musicianship skills. Learning to read music and sight-sing helps establish better musical expertise for singers. Instrumentalists devote quality time in lessons advancing these skills. Singers can and should be taught the musical language right from the beginning of their singing journey. While it is easier for vocalists to learn by ear, instrumentalists begin their studies by reading notation. It is imperative that voice teachers take the time to guide their students in reading and hearing the music they are performing. Theory and ear training can catapult singers into better musical proficiency and procure the assumption that singers are great overall musicians.

CHAPTER 10:
The Five-Step System: Step Four – Vocalizing

The goal is to teach a foundational understanding of efficient singing in a style that young children can comprehend.

After laying the groundwork for mind, body, breath, and musical skills, it is time to move into Step Four of the Five-Step System: Vocalizing. Vocalization exercises are the mechanics of the singing voice. Executing these strategies with children has more to do with rudimental practices than it has to do with voice building. Vocal technique is not just reserved for the adult and teen singers, but for those of all ages who want to learn mastery of skills.

The latest research in voice science has equipped voice teachers with a plethora of knowledge in understanding the mechanics behind singing functions. New methodologies and strategies for cross-training genres are changing and becoming more widely accepted and respected. Singing experts are discovering new methods for training a variety of styles effectively and efficiently through the lifespan, but modern teaching practices still do not universally accept strategies for teaching children; there is concern about damaging the young voice.

Discovering, Learning, Growing

The teacher must choose an approach carefully. Indeed, not all vocal methodologies are suitable for the young singer. In the classical singing world, most teachers develop a style of tone production based around acoustic resonance, training the singer to project the voice and achieve the "singer's formant." Working to acquire this style of singing requires execution geared to achieving a specific acoustical sound.

Other styles, including pop and musical theatre, are also focused on achieving a specific sound. These styles of singing are commonly the most desired by young singers because contemporary pop and musical theatre are the genres of music young singers ordinarily hear first on television, radio, and the internet. Disney songs from hit movies can be quite influential for very young children. Any type of singing where a child is imitating an adult sound can lead to vocal issues and misuse of the voice. In addition to imitation, there are concerns of cultivating these sounds with too much intensity and duration, which could potentially cause harm to a young singer.

Teaching children to sing does not need to fall under any one method, technique, or style. Young singers need to learn necessary skills while maintaining an age-appropriate ability, along with suitable intensity and duration limitations. Regardless of methodology and genre specific teaching, the goal should be to achieve an efficient, lovely sound that functions with ease and clarity.

As children go through puberty, many things will adjust as their physical development changes. It is up to the teacher to preserve the young singers' ability to sing with flexibility and sensitivity. Unfortunately, many parents and even teachers can unintentionally exploit a child's talent when they can make exciting sounds and perform like grown adults. Children need to be supported with age-appropriate technique as they develop. Let's encourage kids to sing like kids. Do not think of children as "building" their voices, but *discovering*, *learning*, and *growing* their young voices.

In beginning to work with child singers it is important to establish an awareness of tone production and find the different ways their voices can make sound. As mentioned in the previous chapter, there are three parts that make up every instrument: The starting point (or generator) in the lungs where the sound prepares with breath, the launching point (or vibrator) where the vocal folds make soundinside the throat, and the resonator, which amplifies the sound and travels to create buoyancy of tone. The singer's goal is developing these three parts to function with ease.

Resonance and Phonation

Coordinating the vibration and resonance needs to start with voice registration. The first technical strategy to focus on is the ability to sing with a light mechanism (head voice) and a heavy mechanism (chest voice). Not all young students come to lessons with these facilities in place.

There are many debates among teachers regarding the variety of ways in describing the interaction of resonance and phonation. Modern research has led us to a better understanding, and many teachers teach a "fact-based" foundation. It is best to keep things simple in guiding children in the concepts of *discovering, learning*, and *growing*. For clarity and recognition when working with children, use basic descriptions about the functions their voice produces. Words like chest voice and head voice are less complicated for children to comprehend. This book is not intended to focus on the science of vocal fold vibration and how it correlates with vocal tract resonance, however, it will hopefully inspire teachers to discover the basic aspects of vocal function. My initiation into this discipline was rooted in the tradition and wisdom set forth by William Vennard. His in-depth look at how the voice works was inspiring and comprehensive. While teachers do not need to be experts in voice science to teach singing, there is power in knowing as much as you can about how the voice works. As Vennard (1967) states in his book *Singing: The Mechanism and The Technic*, "The more the teacher knows, the better." When working with the child singer, the instructor should keep technical information practical and straightforward. Take the knowledge and simplify the instruction into child-friendly tactics, so the teacher has a principle in what they are teaching, and the child has fun singing.

A child can easily understand that their singing voice makes different qualities of sound regarding high/light sounds and low/darker sounds. When teaching fact-based singing, kids can also understand that lower-pitched sounds don't come from a lower part of the body, but they can sound more rooted in the chest. These sounds come from a combination of things and involve the vocal folds vibrating with more thickness. Some interested children enjoy seeing pictures and diagrams of the vocal mechanism. Working with curious young students is inspiring. Their young minds are open to so many possibilities. Just be cautious that kids want to sing, not to listen to a teacher's dissertation on open and closed phonation. Instilling some basic understanding is all they need to develop a good sense of singing technique.

Proper technique is a vital step to promoting the long-term benefits of healthy, beautiful singing. Children have a lack of inhibition and willingness to explore. Their potential for freedom of tone and expression comes out easily, because they don't have preconceived notions regarding failure. Children are more willing to experiment than older singers. Cross-training and offering a variety of styles is also essential in the formation of good habits and in finding authenticity in their unique ability. If more voice teachers developed technique and cultivated efficient singing early on, we could potentially protect young singers from technical failure resulting from misguided or un-guided singing.

A Top-Down Approach

The first step to accomplish in vocalization exercises is strength and coordination. The student must discover and balance their vocal registers. Children need to begin with a top-down approach, meaning they need to strengthen and become familiar with their head voice register first. Most beginners have a strong sense of chest voice resonance because of where their speaking voice vibrates, but they may not like their head voice because it sounds weak and breathy, and they are probably not aware that they can sing in different registers. Thus, in each lesson, the vocalizations should start with a light head voice tone before heavy singing, so that this range becomes more familiar and comfortable for the singer.

In one of my large group singing classes, I taught a ten-year-old girl named Ishana who had a lovely but limited voice. She had no upper range and no head voice access to her sound. Everything she sang was produced in her chest voice, which she tried to carry up in her vocal range. She struggled to sing anything above C5. While it is challenging to guide individual singers in a large group class, I make it a goal in every group session to introduce head voice sounds and singing. I use poetry, call and response, echo songs, and vocal warm-ups using glides and expression lines (these strategies will be broken down in Section III of the book). It is great when a singer discovers their head voice for the first time, adding a new dimension and strength to their sound. Ishana developed a lovely soprano voice with depth and pliancy. After further study, it was inspiring to hear her floating high notes and recalling a time when she didn't want to venture out of the low resonance of her voice.

Another student, Katie, was working on "Over the Rainbow," a song with demanding range and interval jumps. These factors can become even more complicated if the singer wants to belt it or attempt to sing it all in one register. Like most kids, Katie didn't prefer singing in her head voice and favored the strength of her chest voice. We continually worked on developing flexibility with the balancing of her registers. When she first started working on "Over the Rainbow," she attempted to sing it with a heavy, loud sound, until she couldn't carry the sound up the octave with the same amount of ease. We worked to incorporate a lighter resonance in certain spots and to balance the registers using vocalization tactics. Katie made excellent progress on the song and ultimately sang it with evenness and beauty. At age 9, she was already a master at cross-training her voice in a variety of styles and sounds.

Another reason to introduce registration early on with young students is the chance to solve a combination of problems a beginner can encounter. Some inexperienced singers will display pitch inconsistencies, a problem stemming from aural and kinesthetic misfirings. These issues are often a result in the individual not fully grasping what head voice and chest voice feel like. When a singer is better able to understand both conceptually and figuratively how their sound is produced, then they have a better chance of hearing and delivering the correct pitches. In addition to pitch association, singing in a lighter head voice contributes to an easier function and can aid the singer in guarding the intensity and duration of heavy singing.

It is essential to start off teaching young singers by laying a good foundation in the appropriate skill sets. As voice teachers, we can offset some of the faulty technique that singers pick up over the years (especially from modeling their favorite singing idols) and encourage a healthy well-produced vocal tone. In Section III, I will break down the different ages and stages of developmental growth. I will offer vocalization exercises and strategies to use in the area of *discovery*, *learning*, and *growing* in the voice lesson.

CHAPTER 11:
The Five-Step System: Step Five – Repertoire

A song is merely a story told with musical pitches and artistic phrasing.

All the groundwork for achieving technical and musical goals comes together in singing songs. Repertoire is the fifth and final step in the Five-Step System. Singing songs is almost always a singer's favorite part of the five-steps, but it is saved for last because it is the point where the singer can manifest all the newly formed skills together to create a piece of art. Each singer's repertoire is the compilation of songs unique to them. Just like a child's collection of toys, a singer's repertoire is a unique treasury specific to the individual. Choosing the right song, learning the song, and executing a successful performance are the three aspects that go into the "repertoire" step of a lesson.

Choosing the right song

Start building the repertoire with simple melodies that guide the singer in delivering a healthy, and free sound that is unique and all their own. Get to know the student's interests and abilities. Some singers already know a specific song, artist, or genre they like to perform. It is essential, however, to encourage students to venture away from tunes that they already know and into songs they have never learned or heard before. Teaching new repertoire allows the singer to utilize newly formed techniques and not repeat old habits. There is a tremendous amount of beautiful music that spans many centuries and cultures of music. Learning new repertoire guides a student in self-discovery and broadens their knowledge of vocal literature.

Each child is different, and the various ages and stages will render different objectives when selecting a song. For the young beginner just discovering their voice, it is essential to find a song that has a simple melody, moves mostly in step-wise motion, and integrates phrases that are well connected. Songs that contain a conservative vocal range are easy to navigate for young singers and help them to build their skill level. For the very young singer, it is helpful to find song literature that does not contain lengthy text. Most importantly, it should have a great message or story to tell that can relate to a child.

The singer's ultimate goal is storytelling. One of the greatest joys of singing is using the voice to create a mood and expression. A song is merely a story told with musical pitches and artistic phrasing.

The collection of repertoire and song choices should be varied and diverse for young singers. Try to avoid intense and heavy singing with young children and continue to help them discover their unique sound. Just because a child can belt out "Let it Go," it doesn't mean they can pull off all of the nuances in that song. Allowing a young singer to perform songs out of their comfort zone occasionally is ok from time to time, but teach them to respect and honor their current stage of development. There are too many expectations for kids to sing like adults. Moreover, even if they can pull off all of the vocal elements, it doesn't mean they should sing exclusively in that style. Empower young students to discover their unlimited potential.

Another intention for children is to learn songs that have lyrical phrases and legato lines. Much of commercial music today lacks the lyrical qualities that promote beautiful singing. There is also a current trend in commercial music to use glottal fry and a tendency to sing with raspy, broken phrases. This type of singing does not promote healthy tone production, especially for young, growing voices. Because of its popularity, however, I have experienced many a young singer come to me with the desire to insert this faulty technique into everything they sing. Young singers need to understand that these stylistic techniques are conducive to certain genres, but certainly not to all, and they do not help to develop a healthy technical foundation. It can even be unappealing to the listener who is not expecting such a musical style; I once heard young singers performing the sacred parts of the Catholic mass in a traditional service using pop inflections!

In the voice studio, instructors should gently and slowly allow singers to discover all the things that their voice can achieve without the influence of stylization. Encourage cross-training in a variety of styles and techniques; this will enable the student to discern which methods to use in each style and genre.

Allow a singer to work on a favorite song that you may find vocally unfavorable, and then introduce them to a song with a lyrical quality and suitable range. The singer will often discover how much more ease and beauty their tone can produce in an easier song. It is rewarding when young singers have powerful "Aha!" moments about their singing Most popular songs are very lengthy in form and text and are not condensed well for children. In addition, most contemporary commercial music has content that is not appropriate or natural for children to convey. Finding songs suitable for a particular voice is a challenge and a significant part of the job as a voice teacher. Below is a list of some suggestions to look for in a choosing repertoire for children.

- Expressive lyrics that the child can relate to at their young age

- Vocal range (depending on the singer's current ability)

- Tessitura (where the majority of the notes lie in the singer's range)

- Amount of words to memorize (short form)

- Words that the singer can pronounce and understand

- Lyrical lines moving mostly in step-wise motion

Sometimes it may be desired to choose a song that challenges the student, extending the vocal range or teaching new vocabulary. Cultivating a growth mindset helps develop the whole child and not just the singing voice.

Risks are involved with inappropriate repertoire choices. If a child picks a song that is too advanced vocally, it could cause vocal injury. If a song is too challenging, the student could lose confidence in their ability to successfully execute the song. It is the teacher's job to help the student feel valiant in their skills, no matter what level they are working towards in their lessons.

While many children love singing their favorite pop tunes, and often dream of singing contemporary songs at big venues, they would also be happy to eat ice cream and candy all day, while never eating any vegetables. As guardians of the child's voice, the teacher should introduce young singers to a variety of repertoire that will help guide and nourish their growing voice. It is fine to allow them to sing their favorite pop songs, but do not make this the sole focus of their repertoire. Just like dessert, it is a special treat, not the main course. Keep their repertoire choices balanced and healthy.

Singers of any age can lose interest very quickly when not emotionally connected to their songs. For that reason, it is necessary to choose pieces that help meet the student where they are at emotionally as well as vocally. If a singer is forced to sing a song they don't like, chances are they will quickly lose interest in singing lessons altogether. It is important to keep students motivated by giving them some choices in the selection process. Use a questionnaire sheet at the start of lessons to get to know each student. Perhaps they have other interests that can guide the teacher in ideas for connection on a different level. For example, it seems that all girls under the age of ten love any song about animals. Little kids love to sing about cats, dogs, bunnies, and dinosaurs. The better you know your students, the easier it will be to pick songs that they will enjoy. Just remember to encourage variety.

I have witnessed firsthand adverse outcomes from over-singing of strenuous repertoire. Several years ago, a high school student named Krista reached out to me for lessons. She had recently received a diagnosis of bi-lateral vocal polyps. Learning of her singing history, I realized her past was what led her to the current situation. She started taking voice lessons at age eight and had sung pop songs and contemporary commercial music repertoire exclusively. She regularly performed these songs at high profile community events. Most of her repertoire was not suited to her young voice range and ability. She confessed to feeling vocal fatigue and strain over the years. She was often performing in outdoor venues in cold weather and on big stages. She was using too much intensity and duration throughout the performances. This sort of singing is not in the young student's best interest. I recommend this motto for teaching children: *Keep intensity and duration in check.*

Krista came to me looking for a better technique that supported her mission of singing with a healthy and free sound. We reworked her singing technique together with her doctor and her speech-language pathologist (SLP). After a few years of gently learning how to sing with more efficiency, Krista went on to perform a wide variety of repertoire and genres. She is currently having great success knowing how to pick appropriate songs, keeping a balanced and secure technical facility, and understanding vocal self-care. Krista is still happily performing lead roles in many musicals and has a well-supported free sound. I am proud to say she is singing beautifully and is a master of cross-training her voice in a variety of genres. If she ever finds herself in trouble again, it will be from too much intensity and duration.

How to learn a song

It is recommended that teachers begin a new song with young singers by breaking down the learning process into small tasks. Taking the song apart can enhance the technique the child is currently working toward in lessons. As previously discussed, a student shouldn't solely learn to sing by ear. Developing an ability to read music and break down the song into different parts is comprehensive in the nurturing of a well-rounded musician. Begin by listening to the song and then speak through the text. Next, have the singer vocalize the melody on a single syllable or use a kazoo to find the notes without having to sing full voice. The purpose of vocalizing the melody without text is to guide an open and free tone production that is balanced with the breath, which can simplify the note learning process while enhancing breath techniques. Occasionally a singer learns a wrong note or creates tension when reaching for a specific pitch; it can be easier to fix these problems without the words, and it instills good technique.

Once they are secure on singing the melody alone, work on speaking the text with articulation and projection. Discovering how to broaden and articulate the words will bring more presence to their sound. Ask the singer to read the words alone, without regard to pitch or rhythm, so that they can discover the meaning of the piece. The student may find new words that perhaps they didn't know before while achieving an understanding of the context. In addition to vocal skills, studying repertoire can teach a singer many things, including history and beauty. It can also enhance a child's empathy and discernment for the world around them.

Learning a new song through a variety of strategies helps promote mastery of skills. If a student does not study the song with a process of learning, they may go through the motions, learning by ear and not fully absorbing the piece. In many instances, this can cause them to feel unprepared for a performance. It also does not tie in any of the musical and vocal techniques they are learning.

One of my former singers, Izzy, was mostly learning her songs by ear. She didn't take the time to learn the song musically or artistically. She would get frustrated with little mistakes and rarely felt a sense of accomplishment. Each week she wanted to sing a different piece. She resisted my course of action and as a result, seldom mastered any skills. Izzy didn't last long in her interest in singing lessons because she wasn't making any progress and never practiced. I became her accompanist and not her voice teacher.

Guidelines for the learning process will be outlined in Section III, where I elaborate on each developmental category. When a young student follows the guidelines, there is a much better chance for growth and accomplishment than just the task of singing a song because it is fun. It is crucial to make the process of learning exciting while promoting the skills to make it joyful and inspiring. One of the great rewards of teaching songs in this way is that the student not only builds on the foundation of proper singing technique, but they are increasing their knowledge and creating a varied collection of repertoire.

Executing a good performance

Bringing a song to life and preparing for an assessment or performance is the final objective. A student can develop a polished piece in a variety of ways. Work on:

- Memorization

- Dramatic interpretation

- The ability to tell the story using gestures

- How to "slate" (see sidebar) for the performance

- Executing a graceful bow

- Ways to project the sound

- Where to look when singing to an audience

Some performance opportunities might include: a studio recital performance, a community engagement event, competition, audition, or just an in-studio assessment. If a student is learning a song with no immediate performance opportunity, work towards the goal of having the song performance-ready by doing an in-studio performance, or make a video recording to share with family and friends. The guidelines found in the Appendix can be used for in-studio evaluation. You can also make up your own fun and inspiring assessments with the key points you are working on in your studio.

Slate is a common term used in the performing industry for a performer's self-introduction at an audition, performance, or project. It is useful for young singers to begin a performance by stating their name and the title of the piece they are to perform. Slating is an opportunity to learn poise, and it is a helpful moment for the student to prepare their mind and body for what they have ready to share with the viewing audience.

Summary

The singing of repertoire is the final stage in the five-step system and finishes out a well-rounded lesson curriculum for beginning young singers. The next chapter will discuss how to approach lesson structure when dealing specifically with performance preparation. There are times when a particular circumstance or an imminent performance is on the horizon, which require full attention to prepare. Whatever the case, we will examine further the ways to bring repertoire and performance skills to life.

CHAPTER 12:
Mastering Performance Skills

"Practice isn't the thing you do once you're good. It's the thing you do that makes you good."
                                                              —Malcolm Gladwell

Recitals and auditions are just some of the exciting performing opportunities your students will encounter. While you have organized your lesson structure to teach a well-rounded curriculum, there are times to veer off that path and concentrate more intensely on the performance aspect of singing. Encouraging your vocalists to get involved with these occasions is a great way to put all of their singing skills to work. When a performance is approaching, the lesson pacing might require full attention to preparation.

The best strategy for preparing young singers is to anticipate the many aspects that go into a skilled performance. If a child is unprepared for any presentation or singing opportunity, they can feel vulnerable and insecure. The result of a failed performance can leave the singer discouraged. Many of my adult students have told stories of unsettling experiences when they were younger. The outcome left them feeling demoralized and led them away from singing.

Teaching a young student about the many practices that go into a skillful performance takes time and patience. A satisfying achievement doesn't always render a perfect performance. By teaching students to have a meaningful outcome, we can empower them to feel confident and brave for each accomplishment. Preparedness is key for their success, and it's important to understand that varying circumstances require different kinds of preparation. The diversity of performance opportunities can include annual studio recitals, in-studio assessments, recording session for online and video submissions, community engagement performances, competitions, staged musical productions, and auditions. Each opportunity requires different preparation.

Recitals

When refining a piece for a studio recital, give students plenty of time to make sure the piece is ready. They should follow the guidelines set forth for learning the song slowly and carefully. Undoing mistakes is often much harder than learning the song from the beginning. Emphasize that the piece should be studied so well that they could sing it in their sleep. The nerves and insecurity that arise in various concert settings can distract even the most polished performer.

Recently a group of my students performed at an outdoor festival over a holiday weekend. The performance was in a bustling downtown area, with train tracks running right through the middle of the event. Inevitably, a train plowed through, blaring its horn and whistles, as a young singer performed "Do-Re-Mi." For several measures, the poor young singer couldn't hear her accompaniment or be heard singing. But she persevered and kept going. It was a fantastic experience of resiliency, showing how efficient practicing could serve in the hardest of challenges.

It is also very important to create muscle memory, by taking careful steps in the learning process. Kids can speak the words dramatically; not all rehearsing has to use the singer's full voice. Children can attain an ability to use "audiation" by way of thinking and hearing the song in their head. Ask students to listen to their piano accompaniments while "thinking" about their singing. Performing along with the accompaniment tracks and mentally going through the music are both useful for committing the song to memory.

Another way to have fun establishing useful techniques is to act out the song using imagination. Use props and fun toys to encourage creative thought. These gadgets are great for initiating characters. Invite the singer to sit or move about the room as if they are in a make-believe scene. When the singer can imagine the action taking place, it guides them in their storytelling ability. A student should know a song so well that they aren't thinking about what comes next or about their technique. The muscle memory should take over while telling the story and sharing that with their audience.

The performer should learn the song solidly enough so that if they do make a mistake, they can react quickly. Any little blunder requires a performer to use their insight to assess and recover. It is a privilege and a wonder to watch a young performer problem-solve in the moment and triumphantly utilize their executive functioning skills in a performance. Teachers need not engage in their own fears and stress when a student makes an error in performance. This too is part of the student's learning process, and the young singer may look to the teacher for encouragement and guidance.

In the last lesson before a recital, students should practice singing a mock-performance. The singers must have an idea of where to direct their focus. Have them pick a focal point. Young kids can get very distracted, and their eyes will wander all over the place. Helping all singers know how to sing to an audience is the last step in refining a song. Preparing diligently in as many ways as possible will give students the best chance for success, aiding in calming nerves, memory retention, and a confident performance.

Studio

The addition of in-studio performance opportunities has proven to work well for busy families and teachers. Not all students are comfortable with competitions, auditions, and large studio recitals in the public arena. Offering occasions to learn a song for a performance inspires growth and victory. Adding assessment and recording sessions to your in-studio lessons allows for this to happen. With modern technology, it is now quite easy to make a high-quality video at home. Teachers can now enter students into online vocal competitions, as well as make online recitals. These outlets encourage a student to prepare a piece and refine it for a performance that doesn't require a live audience. Additionally, making recordings and watching them will help guide the singer to a different place of awareness and mastery.

Recently I had a young student who was extremely anxious about performing in the annual studio recital. I invited her to sing in our group piece at the concert and to polish her solo song for an in-studio recording. I had her learn the song just like she was preparing for the live performance. I asked her to dress up, and in her lesson we recorded the song for her family to watch at home. We uploaded the performance to a private YouTube event. She attended the studio recital to sing in the group piece and realized she was more confident than she thought. Following that experience, she was ready to perform in the next live studio event.

Auditions

Many children love the opportunity of performing with other kids, but securing a spot in a choir or musical will most likely require an audition. These tryouts leave the child desiring specific outcomes. Supporting the child through the result is a pivotal moment in the studio for the teacher. Sometimes the parents contribute to added anxiety for the child by being overly assertive (perhaps the "overly-pushy parent" on p. 25). In any case, it is wise for the teacher to be supportive and help the singer to engage in the experience of the audition rather than focusing on the outcome. The main emphasis with children should be promoting confidence and emphasizing a feeling of courage and perseverance. It is always good to remind the student of the process, that studying singing is an ongoing journey and not a final destination.

Musical Theatre Auditions

Requirements for theatrical auditions vary for each organization. Every theatre and every show has a different set of rules. One theatre might ask a singer to sing a song from the specific show, while another organization might ask them to sing a designated 16-bar (or 32-bar) cut from a song that best shows off their ability. In any case, the song selection is usually of similar likeness to the character or role they hope to land in the production. There are many nuances to theatrical casting and most likely will include an acting and dancing call at the tryout. If young singers will be spending a great deal of time cultivating theatre auditions, it is in the teacher's best interest to gain as much information as possible about the process. In addition to choosing monologues, students will need help in acquiring good headshots and resume formatting.

Audition coach Kurt Domoney of Broadway Kids Auditions in New York City recently shared his advice with me about preparing his performers for auditions. He said that having an audition coach who knows what the local industry is looking for can be very helpful for singers wanting to cultivate something beyond the voice studio. He sees many mistakes young performers make when arriving to auditions, by singing in the wrong style or with their music in the wrong key. Kurt said that while transpositions of some songs are OK, transposing others is just not acceptable because of the uniqueness of the vocal range specific to the role. Another aspect of preparing for auditions is organizing cuts in the musical score to meet the requirements of audition timing. For studio teachers who are not familiar or comfortable with the specifics of musical theatre audition preparation, a knowledgeable audition coach can offer highly valuable insight that complements the voice lesson curriculum.

Girls and boys can also be led by a trained audition coach to try something refreshing and different. Kurt once had a boy sing "Maybe" from *Annie*, auditioning for a role in *Oliver!* A performance that shows off an interesting, fresh quality can appeal to casting agents seeking originality. Kurt says that the agents are seeing a lot of the same thing and the talent level is high. Having kids bring uniqueness to the audition, while keeping up with the expectations, is key to success.

Singers who are routinely and actively pursuing a career as a child performer need to have more specialized attention in the arena of preparation. The voice teacher can handle an occasional audition within the voice lesson curriculum. However, children looking to gain full exposure in the professional industry may need specialization that requires an acting and audition coach so that the voice teacher can devote specific time to singing and musical technique. Know your niche as a voice teacher, and direct your students wisely.

Choral Auditions

Requirements can also vary in auditions for a local children's choir. Some choirs may only request the singers to perform "Happy Birthday," while others may ask to prepare an art song and monologue, or poem. A choral audition typically includes vocalization exercises to determine the child's vocal range. Reciting a monologue or poem helps the director measure the acting and speaking quality of the child's voice. Helping the young singer to be adaptable at hearing new exercises and scale patterns can be helpful and make the student feel more confident in their ability to sing on the spot. Choral auditions may also include some theory and ear-training samples to assess proficiency

Sometimes the desired outcome is that the child gets cast in a show or lands a spot in the children's choir. Be aware that these opportunities will most likely create conflicts in the child's schedule. It is in the best interest of the young singer to maintain their lesson schedule. Stage directors and choir directors are not in charge of each child's voice; voice teachers are the guardians who can safeguard the child's technique and keep intensity and duration in check. Before the audition, make it clear to the parents that continued observation and guidance by the private teacher is highly advised.

in that area. Most children's choirs are looking for voices that blend well. They prefer singers with proper musical training and clear tone production.

Community Engagement

There are several different opportunities for children to perform in their community. It is common to be asked to sing the national anthem at a sporting event or other community event. "The Star-Spangled Banner" is not an easy song for vocalists of any age. It is has a wide range with big leaps and jumps through the vocal phrases, and is usually performed unaccompanied. Preparing for this performance requires work with the phrasing, register balancing within the vocal range, and learning to sing a cappella.

Other community engagement events besides the national anthem could include singing a prepared solo piece at a festival, parade or town hall meeting. These events might involve singing with karaoke tracks, microphones, or with live bands and orchestras.

Religious Ceremonies

In religious settings children may be asked to prepare a church solo or sing as a cantor. It is best if the teacher is well-versed in the different religious traditions and customs to assist in preparation. If the teacher is not familiar with the traditions, try to find out what specifics might be helpful to know. Some of the varieties include cantoring parts of the Catholic mass, solo anthems in protestant churches, solos for contemporary Evangelical services, and weddings. Some teachers may do prep work for bar and bat mitzvahs. Whatever the case, teachers must do their homework or delegate to another expert to help support and guide the singer in feeling confident.

Senior Living Homes

It is a meaningful opportunity for young singers to sing at a retirement community or an assisted living home, and Senior citizens enjoy performances by children. These events teach empathy and charity to our young students. Preparing children for these kinds of performances requires some essential tips on understanding the situations they may witness in a nursing home. A health service environment can be unnerving to some young children. Some of the behaviors, such as loud talking from residents, potential lack of motor function, walking around or leaving in the performance, combined with the ambiance, all have the potential to distract young singers. Adequate preparation for these circumstances will be well worth the effort.

Competitions

Once or twice a year students may perform in local, state, or national contests. Getting involved with national organizations that offer achievement festivals and examinations is a great way to encourage progression, and can be very influential in guiding singers to sequenced development in theory and performance. It is valuable to find competitions that offer positive feedback and reinforcement for growth and development. Each child is different, and parental support is necessary to help guide the student at home in qualifying for these events. The teacher must know what the procedure will be for the evaluations. Prepare the student by doing in-studio assessments based on the rubric.

Most often the singer will be in a room with a single judge who is listening and writing during the performance. The student should anticipate some immediate feedback and or coaching from the adjudicator.

Let the singers know that it is OK to make a mistake, and, if necessary, to start over again. These adjudicated events are designed to help the singer build self-confidence and pride.

Meaningful performances require patience, perseverance, courage, and ambition. By helping young singers to thoroughly prepare, teachers can help them to have an empowering experience regardless of outcome or any mistake. Gaining as many performance skills as possible is one of the main factors for the mastery of singing technique. Organizing lesson structure into a sequence of technical points and developing performance strategies provides young singers with an all-encompassing curriculum. The goal is to encourage children to be life-long singers, performers, and learners in the art of singing.

SECTION III
The Discover, Learn and Grow Curriculum

CHAPTER 13:
Discover Your Voice

"Children have real understanding only of that which they invent themselves."
—Jean Piaget

In this section the Five-Step System is broken down into suggested activities for three distinct age group and development categories. The suggested rubric and activities for beginning singers, ages 5–7 are for **Discover Your Voice** singers. Children this age are just beginning elementary school and are "discovering" all sorts of new things from being independent and exploring new experiences. I refer to children in this category as *Discovery Singers* because they are able to discover the many wonderful aspects of musical education through their own singing voice.

All of the following categories are intended to be a guideline, noting that all kids are different and develop at different ages and stages. These exercises and strategies come from a variety of sources, through my practice in yoga and Pilates, to my work as a singer, voice teacher, and classroom educator. They are continually modified in a lesson to fit each student's needs at the moment. Teachers should be creative and improvise. Feel free to modify and add to each of these exercises to adapt to your own teaching style and to the needs of your individual students. Each task and skill in a lesson should have a function geared toward the child's developmental needs.

1. **Mind and Body Warm-Ups:** Addressing the mind and body first helps the singer prepare for learning. Start the lesson by getting the young singer to focus on the teacher and bring awareness to their body and how it is used for singing. These exercises establish good habits and can be helpful throughout the lesson to occasionally redirect the singer to be "mindful" if they get rowdy and un-attentive. It is not necessary to use all of them in a single lesson.

   • **Stretching:** Movement
     – **Technique:** Get the body moving while bringing awareness to lengthening the spine.
     – **Set-up:** Stand tall.

- **Activity:** Pretend to be Jack and the Beanstalk and climb up to the sky.
- **Tip:** Tell the child to put pretend glue on the bottom of their feet and keep them glued to the ground while reaching higher.

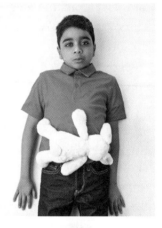

- **Lying Down:** Focus
  - **Technique:** Regulates the mind and body while bringing awareness to breath motion.
  - **Set-up:** Lie still on back and bring awareness to the breath.
  - **Activity:** Ask the child to place a hand or a stuffed toy on the child's tummy to feel the low belly action.
  - **Tip:** Focus on the exhalation first to let go of excessive energy. If possible, encourage the child to close their eyes. Use a stuffed animal for fun and calming.

- **Sitting:** Focus
  - **Technique:** Feel the breath motion in a vertical position and connect with the teacher.
  - **Set-up:** Sitting cross-legged.
  - **Activity:** Breathe in slowly and exhale.
  - **Tip:** Don't let the back get rounded. Sit up tall. This is a great spot to come to for rhythm games and echo activities. Sitting at the same level as the student helps them feel connected to the teacher.
- **Copy-Cat:** Movement and Focus
  - **Technique:** Mindful observation.
  - **Set-up:** Stand facing each other with good posture.
  - **Activity:** "Simon Says." Give the student three movements to repeat back to the teacher. Build up to five actions until they can't remember what comes next.
  - **Tip:** Allow the child to give some examples to the teacher too!

- **Standing:** Posture-Poise
  - **Technique:** Learn proper poise for maximum singing efficiency.
  - **Set-up:** Feet together.
  - **Activity:** Zip the front of the feet apart to make a V, then step the heels open to firmly plant both feet shoulder-width apart.

  - **Tip:** Children will most often over-exaggerate when you ask them to stand tall. The best way to create good posture in children is to tell them to keep their shoulders away from their ears. Use a shoulder buddy prop attached to their shirt to remind them to keep length in their neck.

> **BONUS TIP:**
> *It can be hard for children to stand for long periods. Always allow for plenty of movement away from standing still. The longer a student has to stand still, the wigglier they will get. Allow plenty of moments to move around and then return to good posture and standing still. Do this until they have the stamina to stand in one place for more extended periods. Offering an adjustable stool for sitting can also be helpful.*

What a *Discovery Singer* should know from this step: The young singer should be able to participate with the teacher using focus and responsiveness independently. They should be aware of how the body is used for singing and employ good posture when standing to sing.

Helpful Props: Shoulder Buddy, floppy stuffed animal (see Appendix p. 126 for a photo reference of these and other props mentioned)

2. **Breathing and Posture:** Some of these exercises can be introduced in the mind-body warm-ups. Respiration training for beginning students should be focused on understanding the expansive motion of breath and how it is regulated for singing.

- **Horizontal Breathing**: Breath Motion
  - **Technique:** Experience correct inhalation and exhalation motion.
  - **Set-up:** Lying on the floor.
  - **Activity:** Allow children to put their hands on their tummy and ask them to pant like a dog or giggle. When they do this, the diaphragm engages, creating motion in the belly. When they can feel the rise and fall action in their low belly, ask them to inhale and feel a growing movement in their torso.
  - **Tip:** Try to get children to relax and slow down their breath and brain. Children naturally want to breathe into the upper clavicle area when directed to breathe deeply. Teach them to be patient and allow relaxation to enter their minds. With time and perseverance, they will begin to understand this action. Use a straw to slow down and funnel the air into a smaller stream for inhale and exhale. Put a slightly weighted stuffed animal on the child's belly so she or he can feel the motion of rising and falling. If children practice this kind of breathing at home, they will gain added benefits of relaxation and calming from emotional stress.

- **Vertical Breathing:** Breath Stability
  - **Technique:** Directing consistent airflow to get stability in breath pressure.
  - **Set-up:** Stand with proper posture, holding a pinwheel in one hand.
  - **Activity:** Take a deep breath and blow on the pinwheel.
  - **Tip:** Relaxed shoulders should be the primary focus with *Discovery Singers*. Continually remind the young singer to keep shoulders away from ears. Help the child channel the breath flow to have stability and tonus. Use a shoulder buddy if necessary.

Tonus is not forced or weak, but a constant feeling of stability and balance. When teaching tonus, use a stability ball. Invite the student to push on the ball and feel the firmness. When it gets pushed too hard, everything gets tense. If it is too weak, then there is no energy. Using a pinwheel, the teacher can blow and show how stable airflow makes the pinwheel turn. Not a blast, but a steady stream of air.

What a *Discovery Singer* should know from this step: The young singer should be able to understand how the motion of low breath feels. They should know that the shoulders should stay away from the ears and not heave into the upper chest when inhaling. The singer should understand the concept of stable airflow.

Helpful Props: Shoulder Buddy, floppy stuffed animal, pinwheel, and straw

3. **Musicianship:** It can be useful to employ a workbook series for this category. I use the Full Voice Workbook Series. In addition to the workbooks, it is recommended that the teacher play many singing games with the child to encourage singing together.

- **Call and Response:** Matching Pitch
  - **Technique:** Mindful listening and ear-training.
  - **Set-up:** Sitting on the floor.
  - **Activity:** "Oh My, No More Pie" (Appendix, p.122). Ask the singer repeat after the teacher and echo back what they hear.
  - **Tip:** Sing echo songs or create solfege patterns. Pick short melodic patterns to sing. If the child echoes back at a different pitch, try to match the pitches where they are singing. This is probably their most comfortable range for now.

- **Tonic Sol-Fa:** Learning Pitches
  - **Technique:** Ear-training using the physical placement of the pitches with step-bells and hand signs.
  - **Set-up:** Sitting on the floor, using a step-bell instrument in C major. Label each step with solfege syllables.
  - **Activity:** Introduce step-wise singing using the syllables Do-Re-Mi (ascending and descending) then gradually expand as the child is ready to explore Do to Sol and then the octave Do to Do. Employ the Curwen/Kodaly hand signs. Play and sing the notes on the step-bell instrument together. Have the child sing back the pitches alternating with play and singing using the hand signs.
  - **Tip:** Identify ascending and descending patterns. Use workbooks alongside this activity.

- **Vocal Exploration:** Pitch Motion
  - **Technique:** Help the singer understand the concept of ascending and descending motion, and introduce head voice singing. This is a great warm-up for the voice.
  - **Set-up:** On the floor with a long piece of yarn.
  - **Activity:** Have the child arrange the yarn with curving lines. Using the /u/ vowel, have the child trace the line with the voice, exploring high and low gliding sounds.

- **Tip:** It is best to encourage the singer to start with descending sounds in the head voice range.

- **Beat Motion:** Rhythm
  - **Technique:** Learning to hear and feel the beat motion.
  - **Set-Up:** Sitting on the floor or standing and adding motion.
  - **Activity:** Tapping while keeping a steady beat, chanting "Chop-Chop-Chippity-Chop" or "Engine-Engine Number Nine" (Appendix, p. 123) while maintaining a steady beat.
  - **Tip:** Tap on legs, floor, percussion instruments or other parts of the body. While standing, stamp feet and move arms with the beat. Change the tempo while keeping a steady beat.

- **Learning the Staff:** Notation
  - **Technique:** Discovering how to read music.
  - **Set-Up:** Sit on a stool or the floor using a workbook, write and wipe board, or large staff paper.
  - **Activity:** Learn primary staff, notes, and treble clef.
  - **Tip:** Using a workbook allows the student a visual progression of skills learned and achieved.

What a *Discovery Singer* should know from this step: The student should be able to identify ascending and descending patterns, work on keeping a steady beat with tempo changes, sing and sign solfege (both ascending and descending) alone without assistance. The singer should begin understanding basic notation.

Helpful props: Yarn, tone bells, solfege flashcards, small percussion instruments.

4. **Vocalizing:** Fundamentals in singing skills should be taught in the simplest forms for singers discovering their voice. Children singers should begin to understand all the efficient sounds their voice can make while cultivating a sense of high sounds and low sounds. Introduce head voice and chest voice registers with fun games and exercises. Children this age are not too young to introduce the concept that the vocal folds vibrate together to help create these sounds. Make reference to the Journey of Sound and encourage curiosity about how their bodies work to generate sound.

- **Vocal Exploration Exercises:** Head and Chest Voice Awareness
  - **Technique:** Allow the child to discover vocal sounds using head and chest voice resonance.
  - **Activity:** Read poems that explore a variety of sounds by using a light head voice response alternately with thicker chest voice sounds (see Appendix, p. 125).
  - **Set-up:** Read poems.
  - **Tip:** Isolate the two registers and work on them independently. Using hand puppets or stuffed animals, have the child use the different vocal registers to read poems or create stories.

- **Vocalization Glides:** Head and Chest Voice Vocalizations
  - **Technique:** Feeling the full range of the voice and discover the light. "hooty" sounds at the top. This is also an introduction to balancing registers and smoothing transition points.
  - **Set-up:** Use a straw or /u/ vowel for vocal glides.
  - **Activity:** Draw curved lines to shape the sound pattern on a dry-erase board.
  - **Tip:** Allow the child to stretch their voice as high as it can go and glide down to as low as it can go. Let them enjoy drawing their own curving lines.

- **Vocalization with Pitches:** Head Voice Singing
  - **Technique:** Feeling the full range of the voice and discovering the light sounds at the top. It is recommended to start each singing lesson with light head voice sounds so the student becomes more accustomed to this feeling and technique.
  - **Set-up:** Stand at the piano and use a starting pitch around G4.
  - **Activity:** Singing with piano on a 1-5-1 pattern using the /u/ vowel. Moving up by half-steps, vocalize as high as the singer can go to determine the range and then go back down as far as they can go using the head voice mechanism.

/u/_____

  - **Tip:** Ask the child to hold a prop while singing (a Hoberman sphere or a stretchy band or noodle). Expand the toy with the direction of opening while ascending and release on the descending motion.

- **Vocalization with Pitches:** Head Voice Singing
  - **Technique:** Feeling the free and lyrical quality to their sound.
  - **Set-up:** Stand at the piano and use a starting pitch around C5.
  - **Activity:** Singing with piano on a 5-3-1 pattern using the /u/ vowel. Descend while staying in the head voice mechanism.
  - **Tip:** Ask the child to hold a prop, such as a scarf, and wave it in the air while singing, with the motion of the musical phrase.

- **Vocalization with Pitches:** Chest Voice Singing
  - **Technique:** Discovering the difference between light head voice sounds and low chest voice sounds.
  - **Set-up:** Stand at the piano and use a starting pitch around G4.
  - **Activity:** Sing with piano on a 5-4-3-2-1 pattern using the words "How low can I grow." Vocalize as low as the singer can go to determine range.

- **Tip:** Add movement to keep the child engaged and connecting to the motion of the sound. When vocalizing with children, it is helpful to use a mixture of exercises employing words and vowels only. Using words fosters better diction and is an introduction to speech level singing, while using only vowels helps to create legato phrases.

- **Diction Exercises (Part One):** Articulation and Projection
  - **Technique:** Work to get the consonants more articulate, for more ring and presence in the singer's sound.
  - **Set-up:** Standing or sitting on a stool.
  - **Activity:** Ask the child to follow the leader and repeat /t/d/t/d/t/d/t/ and Tip of the Tongue and the Teeth (repeat 3x) (Appendix, p. 120)
  - **Tip:** Work to get forward /t/ and /d/ sounds that are crisp and articulate. Be aware that many young children can have speech delays. Be patient and allow the mind and body to adjust to this coordination.

- **Diction Exercises (Part Two):** Articulation and Projection
  - **Technique:** Work to get the lips moving and encourage articulation while creating movement with the beat.
  - **Set-up:** Standing.
  - **Activity:** Sing 1-2-3-4-5-4-3-2-1 "Momma made me mash my M&Ms."

- **Tip:** Ask the child to pretend to mash M&Ms in the palm of their hand while keeping a steady beat. Note: If a child has a food aversion or sensitive emotional response to any skill or exercise that you are using, improvise another activity that can create the same skill-building tactic.

- **Expression Exercises:** Singing with Emotion
  - **Technique:** Singing with expression.
  - **Set-up:** Standing and moving.
  - **Activity:** Starting around G4, sing 5-3-5-3-1 singing the words: "I'm real-ly hap-py."

– **Tip:** Change the words to express different emotions, e.g. "I'm really sad/mad/goofy/hungry," etc. The exercise can modulate up or down depending on the emotion chosen. Using a variety of emotions helps the child learn how to sing using different facial expressions and gestures. The child will also discover how each different emotion can change in texture and tone quality. Maybe one is loud, and one is softer. This is an excellent introduction to dynamics and how they are used in singing for expression.

- **Scales:** Singing with a Range of Motion
  – **Technique:** This exercise features a mix of skips and step-wise motion combined with syllabic text, to work on singing scales while articulating the text. It also allows the singer to express joy and sing through their vocal range.
  – **Set-up:** Standing.
  – **Activity:** Starting at C4 sing 1-5-1-2-3-4-5-4-3-2-1 with the words "Yes, I really, really, really love to sing." Vocalize the singer on this exercise going up as high as the singer is comfortable and back down to C4.

Yes,   I   real-ly, real-ly, real-ly love to sing!

  – **Tip:** Use props or movement to help focus and maintain stability in tone. When a singer is paying attention not to the exercise, but to the act of singing as a joyful exercise, they frequently sing out with confidence and ring. On this exercise, the child could use the sphere toy to feel the expansion on the 1-5-1 opening of the 5th. Another helpful prop for this exercise is the scarf, which helps free flowing expression and motion.

What a *Discovery Singer* should know from this step: The student should be able to sing and identify the difference in registers between head voice singing and chest voice singing. The exercises in this category are meant to be "discovery" exercises. The young singer should begin understanding what articulation means and how to pronounce words using clear diction. The singer should also initiate an understanding of how emotion is expressed when singing.

Helpful Props: Stuffed animals, straw, Hoberman Sphere, stretchy noodles, expression cards, scarves. Use your imagination and create your own fun prop ideas.

5. **Repertoire:** There are many beautiful songs for children discovering their voice. The young child aged 5–7 is usually more open to the voice teacher's suggestions when choosing repertoire. As children grow in years and are exposed to more musical genres at home, they become more selective in the songs they like to sing. It is important to broaden a child's musical aptitude by exposing them to many different kinds of music and a wide selection of genres. Making playlists for the child and their family is a great way to introduce singers to healthy singing techniques in a diversity of styles. Hal Leonard offers songbook collections with children singers performing the songs, as well as accompaniment-only tracks. These two listening resources can aid children in discovering the many lovely, age-appropriate ways to sing. Below is a suggested format for choosing, learning, and refining songs for the *Discovery Singer.*

- **Guidelines for choosing songs:**
  - Simple text with contextual themes relatable for a child
  - Vocabulary that is manageable for a child's reading skills
  - Simple AB binary or ABA ternary forms (the lengthy text found in strophic form can be a challenge for many young singers)
  - Avoid songs with long and complicated text
  - Pick songs with the least amount of words to pronounce and memorize
  - Vocal line doubled in the piano accompaniment and a simple harmonic texture
  - Melodies that move in stepwise motion with few leaps
  - Melodic content that stays within an octave range, preferably around C4–C5
  - Avoid songs with mature content and themes
  - Find songs that teach specific skills about expression and articulation

- **Guidelines for Learning Songs:**
  - Teacher sings the song expressively while the child is actively listening. Teacher asks the child some simple questions about the song, which will engage listening skills.
  - Listen to a child singer perform the song (pick songs that are in books with both options and/or find YouTube performances of children singing and other performances, i.e., original movie performances, theatre productions).
  - Sing short phrases and have singer sing back to you (echo)
  - Ask the singer to sing with the teacher (unison)
  - Take the melody alone on a single syllable ("doo" or use a kazoo) if the singer struggles to learn the tune correctly. Make short melodic phrases into a vocal exercise.
  - Speak the text slowly and articulately, employing many of the diction exercises.
  - Teacher reads the text aloud with expressive quality to the student and demonstrates how to bring the story to life.
  - Teach children to "audiate" their songs (thinking and comprehending the music by singing in their head, visualizing and not phonating)

- **Singing Songs with Expression:**
  - Discuss the various emotions found in each song: happy, sad, energetic, funny, etc.
  - Discover how to tell a story while singing and envisioning what is being communicated to the listener.
  - Encourage the *Discovery Singer* to draw a picture of what the story in the songs means to them.
  - Guide the singer to discover new words and individual words that stand out to them in the text.

- **Memorizing the Songs:**
  - Listening to recordings with and without singers.
  - Encourage the parents to support the child in listening to the recordings at least once a day. They can play the song in the car or in the kitchen around the house at home.
  - Speak the text often, while pointing to the words, to remember word order and reinforce their reading fluency skills.

- **Performing the Songs:**
  - **Slate (see sidebar on p. 51):** It is essential to teach singers how to introduce themselves and announce what they are singing. When children introduce their songs well it shows poise, projection, and focus.
  - **Where to look:** Instruct the child where to look when they are performing. This can aid in concentration and etiquette for a performance. Guide them in picking a focal point to sing to, but not to stare with laser vision. This task will be an ongoing skill to master.

What a *Discovery Singer* should know from this step: The singers should learn to perform songs clearly and articulately with the piano accompaniment doubling the vocal line. They should discover the skill of having poise and stage presence. They should be able to sing simple binary, ternary, and one- to two-verse strophic forms. Singers at this level are singing melodies that generally stay within the range of an octave and have lyrical qualities. The singer should be able to learn about the text and how to express a mood or emotion in a song. The *Discovery Singer* should be able to utilize some of the technical strategies learned about singing: posture, breath motion, and incorporating head voice sounds. Most importantly, the young singer should have fun and enjoy singing playful songs.

A Note About Practicing

Parents should be required to attend and take notes at the voice lesson with children in this age group. The parent should guide the practicing at home with their child. During the lesson, the teacher should point out what specifics should be written down by the parent. The key things to achieve between sessions should include establishing a routine and repetition of skills. Reviewing the tasks on the list created in the lesson will promote progress. At home, the parent can assist the student with mind and body tactics. They can help their child practice breathing with the provided props, remembering the techniques used in the lesson. The child can also practice vocal glides and work on their head voice and chest voice sounds. The parent should work with the child on reading their text aloud; reading together is an excellent practice for beginners in improving their reading fluency and language skills. The child can also sing along with the recorded piano accompaniments of their assigned songs. The parent should be welcomed to record parts of the lesson to view and use as reminders.

Setting up a structured practice routine at a young age is valuable for growth and success in the later years. Guide the singer's family in acquiring the time and space in the home for regular practice sessions. The area should be free of noisy family distractions. Another critical practice element for young children is listening to samples. Using a songbook that has children performing examples of the songs, the singer should listen to the recordings every day, in the car, or at breakfast while working on other projects. It is valuable to guide the family into cultivating a good routine and structure in the appreciation of beautiful singing and excellent work ethic at home.

6. *Discover Your Voice* **song suggestions:** Listed below are a few recommended song titles for *Discovery Singers* with ideas for skill level singing.

   • **Twinkle, Twinkle Little Star** (Traditional)
   This traditional song is ideal for the very young singer just beginning to discover their voice. The simple melody is enhanced with a basic ABA form that offers accessible text and memorable lyrical quality. The basic rhythmic pattern offers a syllabic texture with the text. This song is perfect for the beginning singer to add physical movement and has a simple range. It can be easily transposed to any key and offers the ability to teach it a cappella at first, then accompanied with melody, or played with a chordal structure: either block chords or arpeggiated.

   • **Do-Re-Mi** (Hal Leonard: *Solos for Kids*)
   This song is a favorite among young singers of many ages and stages, and is great to introduce as the singer learns solfege syllables in their musicianship skills. The melody stays within the range of C4-C5 and moves in a lyrical, syllabic, and simple rhythmic pattern. The binary form is easy to memorize, and the words are fun. Most young children love singing this song while employing the

Curwen/Kodaly hand signs. This movement makes it easier to remember the word order and makes it enjoyable.

- **How Much Is That Doggie in the Window** (Hal Leonard: *Solos For Kids*)
  The cute cuddly animal theme in this song is always a big hit with kids. The vocal range is C4–C5 and moves in a very lyrical quality adding a few skips to the texture, which adds to the playfulness of the melody. The rhythmic patterns are simple, adding some dotted notes to give bounce and character. The form is easy and does not engage too many phrases of text to memorize. The words have several repetitions in the A section. The storyline is cute and fun. Adding a cute "bark" can enhance the playfulness. Invite the singer to color a picture depicting the storyline in this song.

- **Colours** (The Royal Conservatory: Voice Preparatory Level)
  In this short and lovely song, a young singer learning to read music and vocabulary will find many recognizable sight-words and music symbols. The melody consists of quarter notes and dotted half notes. The text is syllabic and straightforward and offers a few new words to add to their growing knowledge of vocabulary. The melodic texture is supported in the piano accompaniment and employs a triadic structure. The various colors add to the scheme and are helpful for memorization. When learning this song, a young child can use crayons to underline phrases and circle sight-words that they know and can read. This is a great selection to use as an introduction to sight-singing. A young singer will recognize many elements if they are learning theory from the Full Voice curriculum.

- **A Cookie for Snip** (The Royal Conservatory: Voice Preparatory Level)
  With a pet and a cookie as the subject matter, this song could be a hit. This playful selection starts on the highest note of the piece (D5) with robust energy, and works its way through lots of great word-painting (drip-drip-drip—detached and descending motion), which is helpful for story-telling skills. The melody is doubled in the piano and moves in a combination of steps and skips. There are a few spots where the tempo changes and the use of dynamics is a must. It is short and sweet in A-B-A form with the B section offering two short phrases. This song is relatively easy to memorize and is lots of fun!

- **He's Got the Whole World in His Hands** (Traditional Spiritual)
  This song has one phrase with three small variations that repeat and alternate in a simple form, making it friendly to *Discovery Singers.* It is also easy to add hand motions for a kinesthetic connection to the words and music. The dotted rhythmic structure is speech-like in quality and is quite natural to achieve. This texture adds dimension and character to the primary form of this piece. The melodic content has many repeated notes and a limited range of less than an octave. All of these combined attributes make this a great choice for not only *Discovery Singers,* but also older singers going through a voice change who have a limited range or are struggling to balance vocal registers. This song can be sung a cappella, accompanied with block chords, or supported with a full score underpinned by doubling the vocal line.

- **Something Spooky** (*Five Songs for Young Singers* by Lin Marsh)
  Seasonal songs are fun to do when children are excited about a particular approaching holiday, and Halloween is an especially fun season to explore sounds and textures in the voice studio. *Discovery Singers* can pretend to be a ghost and find their head voice, using "growling" monster sounds to discover their chest voice. In this song, there is a fun descending "ghostly" phrase that singers love. It is in strophic verse-refrain-form with a spooky storyline, but the text is very relatable to children

of all ages. The very beginning singer can sing just one verse, adding verses as they are able. This song is also a great introduction to singing in a minor key. Singing descending minor thirds is often very natural to young singers. The minor key, combined with the limited octave range, make this song with more complex harmonies quite easy.

- **Winnie the Pooh** (Hal Leonard: *Disney Collected Kids' Solos*)
Nearly everyone is familiar with and loves Disney songs. The fantasy and playfulness in the Disney theme offer many songs that are recognizable with charming qualities easy for young children to enjoy. This song is based on a favorite cuddly old bear, Winnie the Pooh. Singing this song introduces young singers to the wonderful literary world of Pooh in an upbeat tempo with easy playful words, which describe all of Pooh's neighborhood friends. The playful dotted melodic pattern moves in simple steps, adding in a few easy skips. The song has a slightly longer form starting in 4/4 time and a contrasting middle section in 3/4 time. The range is manageable, and the descriptive text is fairly easy to memorize. Enunciating the text requires the young singer to work on diction and articulation. Bonus: This song helps young singers sing with a variety of expressions when depicting the various characters' personalities. Definitely a song young children can portray.

CHAPTER 14:
Learn Your Voice

"Learning is a treasure that will follow its owner everywhere."
—Chinese Proverb

The suggested rubric and activities for beginning singers, ages 8–10 are for *Learn Your Voice* singers. Building off of the foundation established with *Discovery Singers*, this category could be applied to any age as a basic set of skills. I call singers in this category *Learning Singers*. These *Learning Singers* may have some singing and musical experience. The *Learning Singer* could be older than 8–10 just starting out, or this category can be a starting point for any age singer who is well suited to this skill level. As children continue to develop or start lessons at this age, it is essential to assess the child's development level before starting. Some children in this age group may need to hone some of the skills covered in the *Discover Your Voice* category before digging into these skills.

1. **Mind and Body Warm-Ups:** Kids at this age will generally have better focus than the younger age category, but their attention can waver from week to week. It is always good to start off a lesson by setting the intentions on focus and getting the mind and body working together. While children at this age have more awareness and ability to focus, they may also have a little more anxiety about singing. The teacher should help the singer feel at ease.

- **Stretching:** Movement
  - **Technique:** Allows for flexibility and mobility of the spine.
  - **Set-up:** Sitting on a yoga mat or rug.
  - **Activity:** Cat-Cow. Get into a table-top position with hands and knees on the floor, rounding the back up toward the sky followed by arching the back toward the ground. Hands are under shoulders and knees under hips. This can later be developed as a breathing exercise.

  - **Tip:** Encourage the student to curl their chin into their chest for the cat and then open up the chin by looking up to the ceiling for the cow.

- **Lying Down or Sitting:** Guided Meditation
  - **Technique:** Self-awareness. Improves concentration and relieves anxiety. This exercise draws the child's focus inward and brings awareness to feeling sensations.
  - **Set-up:** Lie still on the back or sit in a comfortable position with eyes closed.
  - **Activity:** Have the student experience calmness and have them bring their attention inward. As a guided meditation, ask the child to squeeze their right fist. While holding the tension, take two deep breaths. Then relax and feel the tension release. Continue exercise with the other hand and then to the feet.
  - **Tip:** Ask the child to notice how their breathing changed.

- **Copy-Cat:** Movement and Focus
  - **Technique:** Mindful listening and observation.
  - **Set-up:** Stand facing each other with good posture.
  - **Activity:** Sing a Tonic Sol-Fa pattern.
  - **Tip:** Encourage the student to use Curwen/Kodaly hand signs. Give the student three pitches to repeat back to the teacher. Build up to five step-wise pitches until they can't remember what comes next.

- **Standing:** Posture-Poise
  - **Technique:** Lengthening the neck and spine. Keeping tall always reminding them to keep shoulders away from their ears.
  - **Set-up:** Stand with feet hip-width apart.
  - **Activity:** Stretch up overhead. Then, bending at the waist, flop over until folded in half.

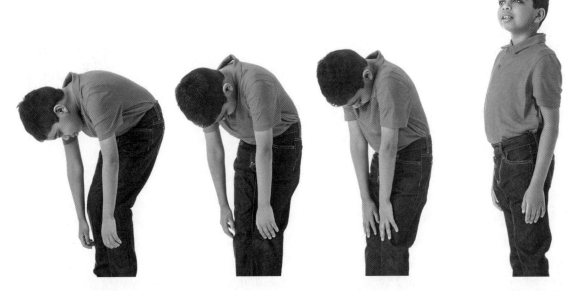

  - **Tip:** With chin to chest, ask the student to unfold themselves as they slowly come to a standing tall position. The chin should be the last thing to come up finding balance and proper alignment.

Bonus tip: Children this age, especially new singers, will get tired from standing too long. Always offer moments to sit and/or move around the room.

What a *Learning Singer* should know from this step: The young singer should begin learning how to draw their attention inward. Teach them to listen to their body and feel sensations. Guide the student to release any anxiety or sensory overload they might be experiencing. One of the best skills a singer must possess is how to be receptive to subtle changes and let go of tensions. Laying a good foundation in understanding these skills is beneficial.

2. **Breathing and Posture:** These exercises can be incorporated into the mind-body warm-ups. Respiration for *Learning Singers* should involve increasing stability in the airflow by not allowing tension to creep into the shoulders or upper chest.

   - **Horizontal Breathing:** Breath Motion and Stability
     - **Technique:** Experience breath motion (in and out) while learning breath stability (tonus) and maintaining relaxation.
     - **Set-up:** On the floor, ask the student to lay on her or his back.
     - **Activity:** Inhale in for five counts and exhale for five counts.
     - **Tip:** Lay a stuffed animal or book on the singer's tummy to feel the resistance on the inhale. Invite the singer to feel the breath motion of the weighted object, while slowing down the breath and brain. Encourage the feeling of stable breath flow.

   - **Vertical Breathing:** Breath Stability
     - **Technique:** Directing consistent airflow without under or overblowing to gain stability in breath pressure.
     - **Set-up:** Stand with proper posture, holding a blow-ball toy in one hand.
     - **Activity:** Take a deep breath and blow on the toy to activate the ball.
     - **Tip:** Help the student feel the core muscles engage. Be careful of overblowing the air, which will cause the ball to shoot out of the basket and onto the floor. The stable airflow will result in the buoyant ball levitating over the basket. Work on getting the breath to sustain for more extended periods.

What a *Learning Singer* Should Know from this step: The student should learn how to feel the difference between relaxed breath and tense breath. The singer should learn how to regulate the breath flow and experience stability that has foundation from the center of their body.
   - **Helpful Props:** Blow-ball toy, stuffed animals or books

3. **Musicianship:** Children learning to sing need a foundation in theory and ear training skills. Employ singing games with the student to inspire and to have fun. Concepts should include steady beat, tempo, pitches, rhythm, and dynamics. It is recommended that the teacher has a dedicated space or workstation (or a hard writing surface if additional space isn't available) in the studio for managing written tasks. A workbook series helps the child engage in written and aural studies.

- **Call and Response:** Matching Pitch
  - **Technique:** Singing by ear and keeping a steady beat.
  - **Set-up:** Standing.
  - **Activity:** Suggested echo song: "My Aunt Came Back" (Appendix, p. 124). Invite the singer to repeat after the teacher and sing back each phrase.
  - **Tip:** For additional skill development, include the motions with this song and move with the beat. Change the tempo and see if they can follow.

- **Beat Motion:** Rhythm Passing Game
  - **Technique:** Learning to hear and feel the beat motion. Singing while keeping a steady beat.
  - **Set-Up:** Sitting on the floor.
  - **Activity:** Singing the song "I Pass the Shoe" (Appendix, p. 121) while passing a shoe (or use any easy-to-manage object) back and forth from teacher to student.
  - **Tip:** Set this game up by first practicing the song while keeping a steady beat. Next, practice moving the shoe by keeping a steady beat. Gradually build to performing the song by adding singing and movement. As the student gains confidence and ability, use a metronome to change the tempo.

- **Ear Training:** Learning Solfege
  - **Technique:** Ear-training; learning to hear and sing the major scale.
  - **Set-up:** Sitting at a workstation using a step-bell instrument in C major.
  - **Activity:** Building on the foundation established in the *Discovery Singer* category, work to introduce step-wise singing of the entire octave scale Do to Do' (ascending and descending) using the hand signs. As the student progresses, give different starting pitches to sing the major scale in different keys.
  - **Tip:** Use workbooks alongside this activity and flashcards.

- **Sight-Singing:** Reading and writing
  - **Technique:** Learn to read notes on the staff.
  - **Set-up:** Sitting at a workstation with writing utensils.
  - **Activity:** Ask the student to learn the names of notes on the lines and spaces in treble clef.
  - **Tip:** Ask the student to practice writing the pitches on the staff.

- **Theory:** Notation
  - **Technique:** Learning how to read a variety of musical symbols.
  - **Set-Up:** Workstation; using a workbook, write and erase on a board or on large staff paper.
  - **Activity:** Learn musical terms and symbols, including dynamics and basic rhythms.
  - **Tip:** Using a theory workbook series allows the student a visual progression of skills learned and achieved.

What a *Learning Singer* should know from this step: Students should learn the major scale using a solfege system and be able to sing the scale using any starting pitch. Singers should learn basic notation of note and rest values, while gaining knowledge of other musical symbols used in music notation. The singer should learn to sing while keeping a steady beat, increasing their ability to change tempos and maintain the beat motion.

Helpful Props: shoe, step-bell instrument, solfege flashcards, metronome

4. **Vocalizing:** Condition young singers to have a good foundation in vocal technique, teaching them how to feel efficient and free in their sound production. Children should learn to be comfortable in their head voice register. The *Learning Singer* should be exploring a variety of sounds and the sensations they experience when producing tone. Cross-train head and chest voice singing with a variety of vocal sounds that children naturally use, and help them incorporate these sounds into their singing in a healthy way. Children this age can learn about registration in regard to head, chest, middle, mix, and belt techniques.

- **Vocalization Glides:** Head and Chest Voice Vocalizations
  - **Technique:** Applying breath motion with phonation and learning about freedom of sound through the full range of their voice, while transitioning through register shifts.
  - **Set-up:** Standing, use a straw, kazoo or an /u/ vowel to do vocal glides.
  - **Activity:** Guide the student through a series of glides to gently warm up the voice and encourage the singer to explore the entire range of their voice.
  - **Tip:** Draw shaped and curved lines on a dry erase board or a piece of paper. Follow the line as they explore with their voice. Begin by using head voice sounds first.

- **Vocalization with Pitches:** Head Voice Singing
  - **Technique:** Learning ease and flexibility in the upper range.
  - **Set-up:** Stand at the piano and use a starting pitch around G4.
  - **Activity:** Singing with piano a 1-5-1 pattern on the /u/ vowel. Vocalize as high as the singer can go to explore the top of their range (an IPA pronunciation guide can be found on p. 115).

/u/_____

- **Tip:** After the singer vocalizes as high as they comfortably go, then descend back to the starting pitch. Encourage the singer to use a balanced onset like the y glide /j/ to avoid glottal or breathy attacks. If the young singer struggles to find lofty head voice sounds, use a kazoo.

- **Vocalization with Pitches:** Chest Voice Singing
  - **Technique:** Learning to sing on pure vowels while transitioning from middle voice range to low chest voice sounds.
  - **Set-up:** Stand at the piano and use a starting pitch around G4.
  - **Activity:** With piano, singing a 5-4-3-2-1 pattern using five Italian vowel sounds /i/e/a/o/u/, starting each pitch with the onset /m/. Vocalize as low as the singer can go to determine range.

/mi/ /me/ /ma/ /mo/ /mu/

- **Tip:** Add movement or rhythmic clapping patterns at the end of each sequence to reinforce musicianship skills by maintaining a steady beat.

- **Diction Exercises:** Articulation and Projection
  - **Technique:** Exercising the jaw, tongue, and teeth helps the singer coordinate all of the muscles used in creating good vocal sound. Learning to articulate the consonants will give their tone more presence, and working with the tongue will bring more flexibility as the young singer develops. Diction exercises are also a great introduction to speech-level singing.
  - **Set-up:** Standing or sitting on a stool
  - **Activity:**
    › Make a "windshield wiper"-type movement across the teeth with the tongue
    › Count the teeth with the tongue
    › Elevator tongue – stick tongue out and point to nose then down to the chin.
    › Tongue twisters (repeat each one three times): Super Singing Sally Sue/Red Leather, Yellow Leather/Mixed Biscuits/Nutter-butter-peanut-butter/ Rickety-tickety-toc. (all of these and more tongue twisters can be found in the Appendix)
  - **Tip:** Encourage the student to engage the entire spectrum of facial muscles. Invite the students to create their own tongue twisters. Explore and have fun with these exercises. They will almost always make the student laugh and smile.

- **Chest Voice:** Singing in the Lower Register
  - **Technique:** Singers learn to use speech in their singing and gain more depth to their sound, while exploring the variety of textures and colors their voice can make.
  - **Set-up:** Standing where the teacher can see the student (It is important to keep your eyes on the student and observe any unwanted tension in head, neck, jaw or shoulders).
  - **Activity:**
    › The first step is to ask the singer to say in a loud, matter-of-fact way: "Oh, no you don't." (These strategies are adapted from *Cross-Training in the Voice Studio: A Balancing Act*, by Norm Spivey and Mary Saunders-Barton, 2018)
    › Next, ask the singer to sing "Oh, no, you don't!" on 1-5-5-1, starting at C4 and extending as high as the singer can go before flipping into head voice.

Oh,   No,   You Don't!

  - **Tip:** Encourage the singer to unleash and pretend to be mad. Nudge the singer to go a little higher. Always encourage efficiency in the tone production and listen for any unwanted straining.

- **Mix Voice:** Finding Brightness
  - **Technique:** The singer learns to explore the variety of textures and colors their voice makes, and this exercise can help mix head and chest voice registers.
  - **Set-up:** Standing where the teacher can see the student.
  - **Activity:** Invite the singer to make a bratty baby sound on "waah." Next, ask the singer to sing "waah, waah, waah" on 3-2-1. Start around A4 and descend to around middle C, or wherever the singer is comfortable without strain.

(bratty baby)

/wæ/   /wæ/   /wæ/

– **Tip:** Help the singer learn about the soft palate by recognizing how that space can be higher or lower when creating different sounds, and there can be bright nasal quality when the palate is lowered.

- **Belt Voice:** Singing with High Intensity Safely
  – **Technique:** Learning how to energize the sound. With chest, mix, and belt singing exercises, do not allow the singer to repeat over to the point of extended duration or intensity. Guide them to learn how it feels, and to do these skills by building stamina.
  – **Set-up:** Standing.
  – **Activity:**
    › First, ask the singer to call their mom in a loud voice ("MOM!") with urgency and intensity.
    › Starting around A4, have them call "MOM!" using speech level singing on pitches 5-1.

MOM!___

– **Tip:** Ask the singer to pretend Mom can't hear them, and they really need her. Encourage the singer to learn about the sensations they feel when performing these exercises. The student should learn how to feel the intensity with efficiency and when to back off when it feels forced.

- **Scales:** Melismatic Singing
  – **Technique:** After the high-intensity exercises, it is good to take the singer back to light and lofty singing as a cool-down. In this exercise, the student is singing on the closed Italian vowel sounds and learning about legato singing. This exercise introduces the concept of melismatic and lyrical singing on the five-note descending scale. Work to achieve smooth connection of each note on the descending /u/ vowel.
  – **Set-up:** Standing or sitting on a stability ball.
  – **Activity:** Singing a five-note scale with pure vowels /i/e/a/o/u/ and pitches 1-2-3-4-5-4-3-2-1. Sing each syllable on the ascending pitch (1-2-3-4-5), descending (-4-3-2-1) on the /u/ creating the melismatic phrase. For singers not yet reading the IPA symbols, it is easy to notate these syllables as me, may, mah, moh, moo. Vocalize the singer on this exercise, going up as high as they are able, keeping open and free. Then descend back down to middle C.

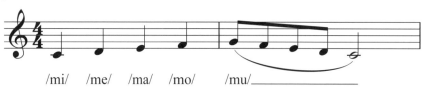

/mi/   /me/   /ma/   /mo/   /mu/_____

– **Tip:** Ask the student to sit on a stability ball and bounce as they sing. This is a fun way to engage the core muscles; it creates a shift in the focus to allow freedom in the sound.

- **Arpeggios:** Extending the Range of Motion
  – **Technique:** Use this exercise to finish out the vocalization warm-ups as a way to extend the range of motion and encourage the singer to unleash and let go. The fast pace and freedom of movement should be encouraged.
  – **Set-up:** Standing or sitting on a stability ball.

– **Activity:** Starting at C4, sing on an /u/ vowel, 1-3-5-8-5-3-1. Vocalize this as high as the singer can comfortably go. Work to extend the range over time.

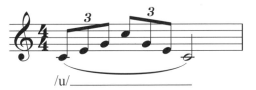

– **Tip:** Encourage head voice and light singing on this exercise. Use an assortment of props to get the singer to open up and engage the core muscles. A stretchy exercise band, stretchy noodle, or Hoberman sphere can help the singer concentrate on the feeling of expansion and resilience. Using props is proven to help children focus and bring their attention to the object and not the anxiety of singing high. If the singer is not yet comfortable in their head voice, use a kazoo to help find the lofty brighter sound.

What a *Learn Your Voice* Singer should know from this step: Young students learning how to sing should begin to understand and navigate the different styles and techniques of singing genres. It is not necessary to utilize all of the exercises in one session. It is recommended to know what each student needs to develop a healthy and free sound and to build their foundational technique from week to week. Regarding kinesthesia, the young singer should learn to perceive differences in forced sound versus free singing sensations. The singer should learn about the soft palate and articulation strategies. Each session should begin with head voice singing, moving into heavier phonation (experimenting with different sounds and impressions) and finish the warm-up with light, lofty singing. This follows the guidelines of keeping intensity and duration balanced.

Helpful Props: Stretchy exercise bands, Hoberman Sphere, kazoos, straws, stability ball.

5. **Repertoire:** Young singers in this age category can get quite picky and particular about the songs they like to sing. As children grow into the mid-elementary years, peer influence and awareness of their surroundings become more prevalent. Find songs kids can enjoy while learning about healthy and artful singing. Introduce a variety of genres and styles. It is OK to allow them to pick a piece that they want to explore that might be deemed inappropriate. Explain why the song might be unsuitable and allow them a chance to try it on and see for themselves. Make adjustments in the text and transpose the key if necessary. Often a child will quickly realize they sound much better on repertoire that is suited to their age and development. It is a must, however, to assign repertoire that is suitable and allows for skill advancement. The pop culture always has a firm hold on the song choices kids are drawn to. As voice teachers, we must introduce a variety of repertoire to balance the artistry and techniques the singer is working to achieve. Most importantly, they should uncover the uniqueness in their own individual sound. Below is a suggested outline of how songs can encourage growth and development of skills.

- **Guidelines for Picking Songs:**
  - Choose songs with lyrics that are suitable for children concerning themes and content.
  - Begin exploring songs with a variety of forms. Progress out of simple AB binary or ABA ternary forms. Children this age are learning to memorize math facts and other information, and are aptly ready to tackle strophic songs with 3 or more verses.
  - Select repertoire that mostly supports the vocal line in the piano but begins to introduce independence and self-reliance of the vocal line.
  - Melodic content for *Learning Singers* should start with easy step-wise motion, gradually adding more fragmented and disjunct melodies.
  - The vocal range can be introduced with simple C4–C5 parameters, venturing into a broader range of B3–E5 or beyond, based on ability.
  - Avoid picking songs that are overly challenging; they can cause the student to force their sound and become insecure about their lack of ability.
  - If the child is picking a song for an audition, the teacher should guide the selection based on specific criteria. (Refer to Chapter 12: Mastering Performing Skills for more information regarding auditions.)

- **Guidelines for Learning Songs:**
  - Make listening recommendations to inspire healthy and expressive singing. Encourage young singers to listen to similar age and level singers, so they are not always modeling and comparing themselves to singers twice (or more) their age.
  - Explore listening examples with a variety of performances of the song (i.e., original movie performances, theatre productions, etc.).
  - Sing the song for the student on a recording that they can practice with at home. For male teachers, be aware that singing in a different octave can be challenging for some young singers to grasp. Illustrate the proper technique you want the student to employ.
  - Sing short phrases and have the singer sing back to you (echo).
  - Sing along in unison with the student.
  - If the singer struggles to learn the tune correctly, take the melody alone on a single syllable ('Doo' or use a kazoo) and make short melodic phrases into a vocal exercise.
  - Speak the text slowly and articulately, employing many of the diction exercises found above.
  - The teacher reads the text aloud with expressive quality to the student and demonstrates how to bring the story to life, without adhering to the musical phrasing.

- **Singing Songs with Expression:**
  - Discuss the meaning behind the song.
  - Discuss the story they are sharing with the audience.
  - Ask the student to write down the five W's for the song: Who, what, why, where, when.
  - Examine the text for new words and ideas that help the singer learn what the song is about, which helps them explore not only the song, but also the world around them.
  - Act out the song as if it is in a scene of a play. Allow the student to move around the studio, pretending to be the character in the song. Encourage interaction with props and furniture.

- **Memorizing the Songs:**
  - Explore a diversity of YouTube performances of the song to gain different perspectives.
  - Practice singing along with accompaniment tracks.
  - Monologue the text and practice speaking by using different inflections and phrasing.
  - Act out the song at home, to kinesthetically connect with the body motions and mentally visualize the storyline.

- **Performing the Songs:**
  - **Slate:** It is essential to teach singers of all ages how to introduce themselves and announce what they are singing.
  - **Where to look:** Instruct the child where to look when she or he is performing. This can aid in concentration and etiquette for a performance.
  - Discuss using gestures and how they are implemented in different genres.

What a *Learn Your Voice* Singer should know from this step: Singers learning about the art of song should be introduced to repertoire that is new to them while also working on familiar songs. Young students should be exposed to a variety of genres and styles to invest in a breadth of knowledge and experience. The singer can employ the skills gained in vocalization exercises by singing songs utilizing head, chest, and mix voice singing, always being mindful of intensity and duration. Singers should begin learning to feel when they are overdoing their sound and when they can give more. They should learn songs that invite them to use expression by incorporating gestures in the appropriate places. Singers this age should also begin looking at the musical score more consistently. Encourage the singers to read the music and understand many of the notational symbols they are learning in their musicianship training. They should begin learning about phrasing and how to mark in breaths.

A Note about Practicing

Begin to create structured practice routines by recording lessons. Students need to become more independent at this age and should be practicing at home by themselves, with some help and guidance from their parents or caregivers. The student should be listening and singing along with the teacher's recorded comments and examples. They should also be listening to other singers perform their solo songs. Young singers this age should be doing some vocalizing at home. It is essential for them to be working on learning their songs (focus on memorization and expressive singing techniques) and reviewing their musicianship lessons. Some vocalization exercises that are good for home practice include breathing exercises, vocal glides, and tongue twisters. It is best not to encourage young singers to utilize heavy and intense singing while away from the trained ear of the teacher. Make notes for what the child should practice and have the student keep a journal. If the student has access to a smartphone, tablet, or laptop, they can make recordings. Some teachers create their own videos for students to watch and practice with at home. Establishing valuable practice habits is an excellent goal for young singers and is a building block of progress.

6. *Learn Your Voice* **Song Suggestions**: Listed below are some recommended song titles for *Learning Singers* with ideas for skill level singing.

- **My Favorite Things** (Hal Leonard: *Kids' Musical Theatre Collection*)
  The text, long loved by listeners and singers of all ages, is fun to sing and allows the singer to learn about articulation. The texture combines lots of step-wise motion and simple disjunct phrasing. The vocal range is ideally suited for young singers and does not employ any high, sustained notes. This is also a great song in which to learn about expression, as the singer must tell a story by depicting each favorite thing. It even offers a chance to change mood and color, which introduces the use of contrasting dynamics. Encourage singers to begin using gestures when emoting in this song. For some young singers, using gestures will be quite natural, while others may find it awkward. Learning to sing a story is always a work in progress.

- **The Wind** (The Royal Conservatory: Voice Level 1)
  Melismatic singing and minor keys are two important lessons introduced in this short song. This piece has a comfortable range of an octave and is best taught using head voice singing throughout the entire piece. Singing in the head voice register makes the melismatic passage more agile. The phrase "woo" allows the singer to perform on the /u/ vowel, incorporating the techniques from the vocalization warm-ups. The storytelling skills in this song are easily adapted because of the beautiful word-painting and mood. The vocal line is not doubled in the piano accompaniment but requires independence on the lyrical phrasing. This song may be short but is packed with great skill-level instruction.

- **The Candy Man** (Hal Leonard: *Kids' Musical Theatre Collection*)
  The young singer can easily examine a combination of registers in this song. The A section melody starts off in a low tessitura that sits around the bottom half of the staff. This allows the singer the opportunity to use chest voice singing. The song has a fun dotted rhythm that makes the melody bright and playful. The ends of the short phrases offer sustained notes with plenty of chances to sing through pure vowel sounds, and the ability to build on breath management techniques. The B section provides an opportunity to isolate and sing in a head voice or mixed voice register, in a tessitura that contrasts with the rest of the song, making it easy for the young singer to maintain a light singing technique. This song also moves mostly in step-wise motion but offers a fun and tricky little disjunct passage that introduces interval leaps.

- **Home** (Hal Leonard: *Kids' Songs from Contemporary Musicals*)
  As a young singer learns to navigate different parts of their voice, this song from the musical *Wonderland* introduces a deeper tessitura. The low range and moderate tempo offer a melancholic atmosphere. "Home" is straightforward in tempo and harmony and moves mostly in step-wise motion. Children learning to read music will find it easy to follow and memorize. The voice part is nicely doubled in the piano to give support of the expanding range that can be weaker in many young singers. Some entire musical phrases sit below the staff and require chest voice singing. The song also requires a balance of register shifts. It is short, simple and very melodious, but challenges the singer to project their sound below the staff and then balance that with head voice singing.

- **Puff, the Magic Dragon** (Hal Leonard: *Solos for Kids*)
  Words and form are the challenge in this iconic song about a boy who grows up and loses interest in his childhood ways. The text and phrases in this edition give the student a chance to dissect the score by color coding and marking up the various verses and repeats. This version introduces D.S. al

Coda, which invites the student to really analyze where they are in the score. The repeats, coda and tempo make this song a bit longer than the average for this age group, but the melody and limited vocal range are accessible. This song can challenge the singer with performance aspects by requiring the performer to keep the energy of storytelling engaging, while remembering the word order.

- **Ev'rybody Wants to be a Cat:** (Hal Leonard: *Disney Collected Kids' Solos*)
When teaching new styles and genres to kids, you don't have to venture too far out of great Disney literature. The jazz elements and arpeggiated melody in this song make it a fun learning piece that kids love. The text is clever and really affords the opportunity to connect to the story line of being a "cool cat," which children this age can relate to. It also introduces some new words and concepts in expression of "thinking outside the box." The range is barely over an octave and the middle section gives the young singer the opportunity to work on mix voice techniques for blending registers.

- **Red River Valley** (Hal Leonard: *36 Solos for Young Singers*)
Folk songs are valuable literature for working on vocal skills and gaining worldly knowledge. Some of the foundational techniques include phrasing, breath management and vocabulary. Folk songs also teach the student about history, traditions, and geography. In this song, the couplets create consistent phrasing and allow the young singer a chance to breathe in between each phrase. Teaching the singer how to write in their breaths and plan for them is an important foundational skill. They can also begin to learn ways to create longer phrases through articulation strategies while building breath stamina. Invite the singer to recite the poetry without musical inflection to feel the structure of the poetry alone. The melodic content in this song also has a beautiful flow and easy form, which makes reading from the score an easy and essential task.

- **Ma Bella Bimba** (The Royal Conservatory: Voice Level 1)
Continuing with folk song tradition and global awareness, this song introduces children to singing in Italian (though it can optionally be sung in English). The text is broken down into just three short phrases that repeat in this swift and spirited song. With its fast-moving phrases, this song is a great learning piece for taking quick relaxed and open breaths. Most young singers will tend to gasp and need to be reminded of how to take in breath with an open feeling free of upper body motion.

CHAPTER 15:
Grow Your Voice

"It takes courage to grow up and become who you really are."

—*e.e. cummings*

The young advancing singer continues to build on the foundation of healthy singing skills and musicianship laid out in the previous age groups. This sets up the young singer for success through puberty and beyond. Children ages 11–13 have more realistic views of life and are more prone to insecurities. Once they start carrying a cell phone, kids will spend time with media on their own, formulating their tastes, while being influenced by their peers. Those exposed exclusively to pop culture are often inspired by a favorite musical artist or genre.

Some singers this age may begin voice lessons as extreme beginners and need to have a foundation in some of the skills previously laid out in the *Discover Your Voice* and *Learn Your Voice* categories. Pre-adolescent singers, or what I call the *Growing Singer,* will generally come to lessons without the assistance of a parent or guardian and must take ownership over their own progress. The pre-teen singers have a better understanding of setting intentions. Teachers need to nurture the young singer to feel confident. With all of the growing changes, it is important to help kids this age uncover their uniqueness as singers and find their authentic voice.

1. **Mindfulness Warm-Ups:** Voice lessons should be a transformative experience for young singers. They should feel safe and secure in their ability to sing for the teacher. These initial warm-ups are designed to help concentration and openness. For older children, the distractions are less often about hyperactivity and the wandering mind and more about the child's hesitancy. Help the growing student find comfort in knowing there are no judges in the room. They should feel free to express themselves and unleash their creativity. Design these warm-ups to bring attention to thinking and feeling. Try not to devote more than five minutes to this category and keep the lesson flow moving. Use these exercises as needed for getting the body and mind ready to sing, and feel free to add your own stretches, applying the same concepts to foster a pliable body and sharp mind.

   - **Review:** Last Lesson Recap
     - **Technique:** Developing work ethic and a growth mindset helps set intentional focus for a good lesson.
     - **Set-up:** Standing or sitting.
     - **Activity:** Start each lesson by asking the student what they learned in their last lesson. Ask them what they practiced and if they had any observations or discoveries.
     - **Tip:** If the teacher uses a practice chart, this is an ideal time to review and discuss what the singer wrote down. Students this age should be working at home without assistance from their parents or caregivers.

   - **Stretching:** Guided Meditation
     - **Technique:** Allows for flexibility and mobility of the spine and gets breath motion started as the student relaxes.
     - **Set-up:** On a rug or a yoga mat.
     - **Activity:** Adding to the Cat-Cow from the previous section, get into a table-top position with hands and knees on the floor. Hands are under shoulders and knees under hips. Add to the movement a breath flow pattern.

- **Tip:** Draw the student into their breath as they inhale while lifting their gaze up to the ceiling for "cow," exhaling as they curl their chin into their chest rounding their back for "cat." Allow this pattern to flow, repeating several rounds of breath.

- **Standing:** Posture and Alignment
  - **Technique:** Lengthening and flexibility of the neck and spine.
  - **Set-up:** Standing with feet together.
  - **Activity:** Stretch up overhead, bringing both hands together, making a fist with the index fingers pointing upwards. Guide the student to stretch up through the torso, reaching to the ceiling, with head and chin in a neutral position. After they lift, bend them sideways at the waist to create a rainbow arch with their body. Come back to the center and repeat on the left side. Come to the center again and gently drop the head back and feel a slight back bend. Continue back through the center, bending over bringing pointing fingers down to the ground. Slowly uncurl the spine as they come back up. Always bring the head up last.

  - **Tip:** Try to keep arms attached to the ears when attempting to bend at the waist.

- **Head and Neck Stretch:** Finding Freedom
  - **Technique:** Aligning the shoulder, neck, and chin.
  - **Set-up:** Standing with feet hip-width apart.
  - **Activity:** Gently rotate the head from side to side and gently massage the jaw muscles.
  - **Tip:** Keep these motions gentle and free of tension.

What a *Growing Singer* should know from this step: The pre-teen singer is developing a sense of freedom both emotionally and physically. Guide the student to be aware of the inner sensations of mind and body while cultivating good posture and alignment. Develop trust and work with the student on how to accept feedback for producing positive change.

2. **Breathing Exercises:** As the *Growing Singer* advances and has laid a foundation of efficient breath techniques relating to freedom and stability, it is time to work on building resilience through control of the airflow patterns.

- **Horizontal Breathing:** Stability and Control
  - **Technique:** Experience breath stability while learning breath suspension and cultivating relaxation.
  - **Set-up:** On the floor, have the student lie on their back.
  - **Activity:** Inhale for five counts (draw the air with the sensation of sipping through a straw), hold for five counts, and exhale on a hiss for five counts.
  - **Tip:** As the student masters five seconds, build to seven, but each round should be equal. Instruct the student to maintain relaxation and freedom on the suspension.

- **Vertical Breathing:** Breath Stability
  - **Technique:** Advancing coordination, building stamina, and gaining more consistent airflow.
  - **Set-up:** Stand with proper posture holding a blow-ball toy in one hand.
  - **Activity:** Take a deep breath and blow on the toy to activate the ball. Use a metronome and count how long the student can maintain the breath flow while levitating the ball. The stability required to float the ball helps to understand the requirement for breath pressure.
  - **Tip:** Be mindful of tension and remind the student to keep shoulders away from ears. Always maintaining good posture. Have the student keep a weekly inventory of the times they achieve at home.

What a *Growing Singer* should know from this step: Students this age should build on the foundation they have developed from posture and relaxation techniques. They should be cultivating more stamina and strength in their breath management techniques.

3. **Musicianship:** Young singers should be developing an ability to read music and learn by ear. The requirements for the twenty-first-century singer include an understanding of written and aural skills. Explore these techniques regularly and be creative in finding ways to make them inspiring.

- **Partner Songs:** Learning Rounds
  - **Technique:** Beginning harmony.
  - **Set-up:** Standing or sitting.
  - **Activity:** Suggested starter song: "Row, Row, Row Your Boat." Sing each of the four short phrases one at a time and have the singer sing it back to the teacher keeping a steady beat. Repeat the song in its entirety and have the student echo the whole song again.
  - **Tip:** Keep a steady beat and as the singer becomes secure and confident work on singing it as a round.

- **Beat Motion:** Clap Back Rhythms
  - **Technique:** Learning to hear and feel the beat motion.
  - **Set-Up:** Standing or sitting.
  - **Activity:** Clap rhythm patterns and have the student repeat them back.
  - **Tip:** Start with a four-beat example, building up to eight beats or more.

- **Ear Training:** Learning Intervals
  - **Technique:** Ear-training – learning to hear and sing arpeggios while beginning to harmonize.
  - **Set-up:** Sitting at a workstation using a step-bell instrument in C major.

- **Activity:** Introduce intervals of a major triad. Ascending intervals: major third, minor third, perfect fourth, and octave. Descending intervals– perfect fourth, minor third, major third, and octave.
- **Tip:** Have the singer sing the arpeggio while you sing a counter-note or melody on opposing thirds.

- **Theory:** Writing Notation
  - **Technique:** Learning how to read what they sing and hear.
  - **Set-Up:** Workstation, using a workbook, dry-erase board or large staff paper.
  - **Activity:** Practice writing intervals of the C major triad.
  - **Tip:** Correlate this with the ear-training exercises and actualize arpeggios on the staff.

- **Sight-Singing:** Singing Notation
  - **Technique:** Learn to sight sing a melody.
  - **Set-up:** Offer a short four-bar melody to sight-sing.
  - **Activity:** Have the student label the notes using solfege, numbers or letter names, and label the counts. After labeling, start by going through the rhythms alone, then chant the solfege syllables with the rhythm. Lastly, have the singer perform the melody.
  - **Tip:** Start with step-wise motion and simple intervals, building off of the skills already taught.

What a *Growing Singer* should know from this step: As singers mature, they should build off of their established notational skills and continue to learn the many facets of melodic and harmonic content. Establish the ability to sight-sing and promote readiness for learning how to sing harmony. Inspire your young students to listen to a variety of musical styles. Expose singers to a broad spectrum of vocal sounds and genres.

4. **Vocal Technique:** Vocalization exercises are the essence of singing technique and can be especially practical for the growing larynx. The pre-teen singer needs to have more intention and exposure to a variety of styles and techniques. Cross training is crucial and necessary to keep a healthy balance for the growing young student. Singers this age are heavily influenced by their peers, through media and pop culture. The *Growing Singer* is physically, mentally, and emotionally maturing, and their larynx is evolving with the rest of their body. Continue to follow their progress and nurture their timid feelings as they transition through the "wiggly" sounds their growing voices will make. As a singer grows, their larynx will increase in size and cause breathiness and uneven tone. Boys and girls will both experience these changes, with boys being affected by more dramatic adjustments due to the bigger increase in size. As the growing student starts to develop challenges in their high range, work to keep head voice singing active through puberty changes. Eventually, they will be able to add more depth to their sound and gain some extension to the range. As they mature, continue to be observant of how much intensity and duration the singer is exerting. Do not let them overuse their voice; guide them to know the difference between freedom versus pushing.

> **BONUS TIP**
>
> *It is not recommended to stop singing when pubertal changes start occurring for boys or girls. Boys' voices will change more dramatically than girls, and the voice teacher must be secure in their teaching practices to handle the changes that can occur. It is just as common for girls this age to experience cracking and weakness in their upper range. For teachers working with this age group, it is advised to have a working knowledge of the mechanics and how and why the changes are occurring. Young voice expert Dr. Jenevora Williams advises voice teachers to practice empathy and help the singer prepare for the changes that are to come. It is highly encouraged for anyone working with a pre-pubertal singer to read as much as possible about the inner workings of the larynx and the changing voice. It is necessary to offer as much emotional and vocal support as possible to these Growing Singers.*

- **Vocalization Glides:** Lip Trills/Vocal Exploration
  - **Technique:** Singing Semi-Occluded Vocal Tract exercises (SOVT). Learning stability of breath while navigating over breaks and singing with lighter vocal fold vibrations.
  - **Set-up:** Standing with good posture.
  - **Activity:** Make vocal sounds through buzzing lips or through a straw. First, start by producing a single pitch and then work on doing glides up and then down through their pitch range.
  - **Tip:** If a student is not able to make a lip trill yet, substitute with a tongue trill, humming or continue phonating through a straw.

- **Vocalization with Pitches:** Head Voice Singing, Part 1
  - **Set-up:** Standing and singing.
  - **Activity:** Sing through a lip trill starting pitch around G4 and vocalize a 1-5-1 pattern ascending to a comfortable range.

- **Tip:** Start slowly in small increments as the singer builds lip and breath stamina to maintain the stability of the buzzing sound. Use a stretchy noodle or prop to distract the mind from over thinking about the lips. If the student is not able to effectively execute this exercise, use another variety of a head voice warm-up on like the vocalization glides on p. 74.
- **Technique:** Learning ease and flexibility in the upper range while creating more stability in the breath.

Semi-Occluded Vocal Tract (SOVT) exercises are commonly used as gentle warm-ups by narrowing the vocal tract and reducing the amount of breath pressure required to phonate at full capacity.

- **Vocalization with Pitches:** Head Voice Singing, Part 2
  - **Technique:** This is another common SOVT exercise. It aids in creating ease and flexibility in the upper range, while developing more stability in the breath.
  - **Set-up:** As an alternative or in addition to lip trills.
  - **Activity:** Using a tall cup of water filled half-full, sing through a medium-sized straw in the water while making bubbles.
  - **Tip:** Don't allow the singer to over-blow. Maintain small bubbles that stay contained in the cup of water.

- **Diction Exercises:** Articulation
  - **Technique:** Encourages freedom of the tongue, jaw, and facial muscles while developing the combination of lengthened vowels and over exaggerated consonants.
  - **Set-up:** Standing or sitting on a stool.
  - **Activity:** Say these phrases out loud: Too Hot, Hot Potato, Potato. Pancake, Pancake Platter, Platter Scatter, sustaining on each vowel sound.
  - **Tip:** Allow the student to engage the entire spectrum of facial muscles by over exaggerating each consonant. Lengthen each vowel sound alternating with the quick and plosive consonants.

- **Mix Voice:** Finding Brightness
  - **Technique:** Singing on a bright nasal sound while building articulation functionality
  - **Set-up:** Standing where the teacher can see the student
  - **Activity:** Singing through the nasal consonants sustaining /i/ and the end of "hang-guhn-nuhm-mee" on a single pitch starting at C4, once slowly followed by three faster triplet repetitions.

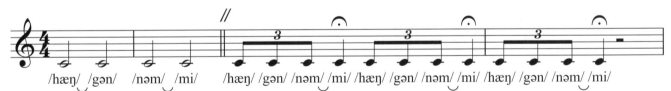

  - **Tip:** Work slowly as the singer gains the articulation coordination for this exercise.

- **Belt Voice:** Singing with High Intensity
  - **Technique:** Learning to sing with thicker vocal fold vibration higher in the range and the ability to discern the physical impact.
  - **Set-up:** Standing with good posture.
  - **Activity:** Following up from the previous belt voice activity in Chapter 14, build with more sounds by calling "HEY, THERE!" with urgency and intensity. Starting around A4 have them call "HEY, THERE!" using speech-level singing on pitches 5-1.

HEY THERE!

- **Tip:** Never allow the young singer to overdo these exercises. Gently guide them to unleash and feel the power of letting go. Teach the student to know when they are pushing and overexerting. Perform these exercises with attention to intensity and duration limitations.

• **Messa di Voce:** Dynamics and Control
  - **Technique:** Coordinates breath pressure by building stamina. Balancing registers and vocal control.
  - **Set-up:** Standing at piano.
  - **Activity:** On a single pitch, start singing pianissimo, crescendoing to forte on a single vowel sound, followed by a decrescendo back to pianissimo.
  - **Tip:** Start this exercise using a light voice to teach a balance of breath pressure. As the singer advances in technique, add a blend of registers including; head, mix, and chest voice singing to balance the intensity shifts of vocal fold vibration.

• **Kaleidoscope Vowels:** Legato Singing
  - **Technique:** Learning legato vowels improves resonance by creating tall space in the soft palette. Develop a smooth connection of vowels using breath stability.
  - **Set-up:** Facing the teacher and standing with good posture.
  - **Activity:** Sing each of the Italian closed vowels /i/e/a/o/u/ on a single pitch. Use an /m/ to create the syllable /mi/me/ma/mo/mu/ on each pitch.
  - **Tip:** Sing each syllable smoothly. Offer a kaleidoscope and ask the student to look into the tube and see the rotation. Visualizing this motion will help the student actualize the smooth connection required for legato singing. While looking into the tube and rotating, have the singer vocalize the exercise again and notice the legato transformation of uniquely blending from one vowel into the other without interruption.

• **Scales:** Melismatic Singing
  - **Technique:** Melismatic singing on the five-note ascending/descending scale.
  - **Set-up:** Standing or sitting on a stability ball.

- **Activity:** Singing a five-note scale on a /u/ vowel. Start with a repeating pattern on the tonic note singing each of the five vowels /mi/me/ma/mo/, 1-1-1-1- singing through the scale on – /mu/ 1-2-3-4-5-4-3-2-1.

/mi/ /me/ /ma/ /mo/ /mu/

- **Tip:** Have the student pretend they are bouncing a ball on the repeated vowels. Throughout the scale, throw an imaginary ball in the air. You can also have them throw a prop up in the air and catch it coming back down. The singer may need the support of the vocal line played along in the piano. Work on increasing independence by dropping the vocal line and playing only chords. Then drop out completely, and increase technique by having the singer perform the exercise a cappella. Discuss with the singer how this must be sung using a lighter voice. The weight of heavy singing will not foster agility in the technique.

• **Arpeggios:** Staccato
  - **Technique:** Learning clean and clear, detached articulation using a relaxed jaw.
  - **Set-up:** Standing at the piano where the teacher can observe
  - **Activity:** Starting at C4, singing rapidly on /ja/, 1-1-1-1-3-5-8-5-3-1.

/ja/   /ja/   /ja/   /ja/   /ja/ /ja/ /ja/ /ja/ /ja/ /ja/ /ja/

- **Tip:** The jaw should hang free, while the tongue creates the action. Ask the singer to gently place their fingers on the chin to keep it from creating tension.

What a *Growing Singer* should know from this step: Students in this age range should be vocalizing at home by themselves. Advise them to set intentions for improvement in their overall sound quality. Have them record each lesson and nurture their practice habits. Spend time instructing the student on how to use their voice at home and in the studio with care. The execution of legato phrasing and melismatic singing should be cultivated, along with belt and mix voice techniques. The student should know the difference between vigorous and gentle voice use and how to practice them differently. Continue using a variety of cross-training strategies that inspire a desire to explore many different styles and techniques. Young singers should be growing while gaining an understanding of their own capabilities.

Helpful Props: Stretchy exercise bands, small ball or sphere, kaleidoscope, straws, cups of water, stability ball

5. **Repertoire:** The study of song literature is essential for young singers. When choosing songs, recognize the style and performance practices in a variety of genres. Pick songs together and allow the student a chance to make some choices by giving them listening options. When the singer blossoms into pre-adolescence, be careful of the desire to assign songs that are mature in regard to content or vocal stamina. It is up to the teacher to protect the growing instrument. Offering a wide diversity of styles encourages young singers to broaden their understanding of singing techniques and guides them to discover their own personal strengths.

- **Guidelines for Picking Songs:**
  - As a singer builds on singing techniques, find songs that adapt to the skills they are developing in their vocalization skills.
  - As the singer advances in musical skills, begin selecting repertoire that incorporates independence of the vocal line in the accompaniment.
  - Select repertoire to balance the many styles of vocal literature.
  - Melodic content can explore a wide variety of textures and articulations.
  - The vocal range can vary depending on the stage and development of the individual singer. Stay within the range of A3–G5 and a tessitura between A4–C5. Be aware of the breaks and changes in the voice.
  - Find songs that the singer is very comfortable singing.
  - Avoid choosing hard songs, thinking that they will grow into it.
  - Select songs that encourage storytelling and pick songs that the child can relate to emotionally.
  - If the singer is confronted with early voice changes, choose songs that can be transposed easily and have limited vocal range.
  - Offer a variety of melodic phrase lengths to build on breathing techniques and interpretation practices.
  - Introduce songs in a different language.

- **Guidelines for Learning Songs:**
  - Have the student explore an array of video and audio performances of the song.
  - Encourage them to learn the song by utilizing their musicianship skills in note-reading and aural skills.
  - Have the singer sight-sing the melody in their lesson.
  - Have the student use their recorded lessons to review for home practice.

- **Singing Songs with Expression:**
  - Ask the student to write down the five W's for the song: Who, What, Why, Where, When.
  - Discuss text painting and capture the essence that a composer might be illustrating in a song.
  - Discuss with the singer that in addition to the composer, there is a poet or lyricist who provides the text.
  - Use imagination, originality, and storytelling tactics.

- **Memorizing the Songs:**
  - Chant the text with the rhythm using mental practice to "audiate" singing.
  - Listen to recorded lessons and accompaniment tracks.

- **Performing the Songs:**
  - **Slate:** Continue with this age group the ability to make an introduction and introduce their song using projection and their own personality.
  - Teach the singer about different performance protocols for the varying genres. Musical theatre songs can potentially require a more dramatic physical approach, using gestures to help tell their story.

Art songs typically require more focus on facial expression. Pop songs utilize more autonomy in expression and in most cases might require a microphone.
– Tell a story and communicate emotion to the audience.

What a *Growing Singer* should know from this step: The student should have a growing knowledge of song literature regarding style and genre (such as Disney, pop-rock, folk, religious, art songs, and musical theatre). They should be working independently at home to listen to and learn their songs. The student should know who wrote the text to their song and understand the different performance practices that are associated with their selection.

A Note About Practicing

Cultivate a growth mindset by establishing goals to inspire and achieve. Note taking, and monitoring progress can be different for an older child, especially if the parent was previously keeping tabs on the progress. When a child is coming to the lessons by themselves, it is an essential task for the teacher to direct what kind of assignments need to be worked on at home and how to manage their practice time. If a child is new to taking notes on their own, have a guideline for teaching this significant task. Encourage note-taking and recording during the lesson. At home, have the student go back over the notes and recordings. They can make notations in a notebook or a dedicated practice journal to keep tabs on progress. The teacher will find it useful to keep personal notes on the development of each lesson with details and expectations. Once the young singer has learned a few songs, advise them to categorize and begin building a repertoire list reflecting the diversity of genres and selections.

6. *Grow Your Voice* **song selections:** Listed below are suggested songs of varying styles for the *Growing Singer* with ideas for performance and technique building. There are so many wonderful songs to choose from and this short list is an example of the variety that can and should be offered.

    • **Swinging On a Star** (Royal Conservatory of Music: Voice Level 3)
    The swinging eighth notes and lilting melody make this charming song a fun adventure in practicing word order and developing storytelling skills. The text is important in the delivery of the message and continues to motivate the singer to practice speaking the text away from the musical phrase to achieve clear pronunciation and inflection. The melodic content has a comfortable vocal range, and registration is easy to manage. The use of accidentals helps the singer begin an understanding of chromaticism, while the disjunct phrases are juxtaposed with triadic movement and big leaps. All of the texture in the song creates a playful and skillful vocal line that is fun and catchy to sing.

    • **Come by the Hills** (Royal Conservatory of Music: Voice Level 3)
    This tuneful Gaelic melody celebrates folk traditions of Scotland, offering a gentle sweeping melodic line with a comfortable range of C4–D5. It is an excellent introduction to folk and art music, with poetry that evokes moods and colors of a bygone era. The words introduce young singers to unique vocabulary and allow for discussion and teaching about breaths within a phrase. The song also has an independent vocal line underpinned by an arpeggiated piano accompaniment. This song is ideal for a growing singer learning to gain independence as a performer. At the beginning of each phrase, the upbeat is led by the singer without piano support, which inspires the singer to be the leader. The lyricism in this piece guides the performer to understand breath

management, while gaining an understanding of word painting. The gentle rise and fall of the melodic line evokes the ambiance of rolling hills and young singers can begin to understand how composers create artful expression through melody.

- **Over the Rainbow** from *The Wizard of Oz* (Harold Arlen)
Singers of all ages love this beautiful standard of vocal literature, and the skills required can be a good challenge for young singers. There are a few nuances to execute with the vocal range, especially if the singer learns the song with the original lost verse not heard in the movie version. Teaching this song by acquainting the singer to the original introduction is helpful because it sets up the storyline and offers and a new and unique perspective. Some younger singers will find the opening section challenging, with the last phrase spanning over an octave and a half. Because of its wide range, this piece is not easy to transpose. Singing the wide leaps can also be challenging to achieve with the lilt and stability of tone. Nonetheless, it is a great song to enjoy and use for instruction on legato phrasing through a disjunct melody.

- **Longing for Spring** (Hal Leonard: *36 Solos for Young Singers*)
This song by Mozart is a wonderful introduction to the sophisticated music of the European classical period. The melody offers a chance to vocalize on melismatic phrases and begin singing ornamentations with a quick mordent at the end of each verse. The piano accompaniment supports the singer with an arpeggiated foundation, which guides the singer to create legato phrasing. The text introduces young singers to many new words that are not in their typical vocabulary. In contrast to articulating the text, the young singer must incorporate the "kaleidoscope vowel" technique and work on singing through open and pure vowel sounds to create the smooth line of each phrase. The performer must also sing the three verses with an understanding of dynamic contrast.

- **Vaccai Practical Method of Italian Singing** (Schirmer's Library of Musical Classics)
The Vaccai Method is perfect for the growing singer ready and eager to learn a more formal style singing. The method includes integration to musicianship skills evolving from the major scale, singing in steps, and gradually developing interval understanding and ultimately learning many of the ornaments used in Bel Canto style singing. As the method progresses in musical skills, it also introduces Italian text, which uniquely syllabifies each syllable to end on a vowel. The strategy helps the singer achieve smooth phrasing by connecting the final consonant of each syllable to the next syllable. This technique is ideal for developing legato singing and enhancing vocal resonance in the classical tradition.

- **Round-Shouldered Man** (Hal Leonard Publications: *The Singer's Musical Theatre Anthology: Children's Edition*)
As children get older, it is good to explore gender-specific roles and characters. There are always more songs for girls at this age than there are for boys. While some children identify as gender-neutral, it is OK to think outside the box. This song is ideal for a young singer looking for a male character to sing. Before a young boy begins his voice change, he should be able to navigate through his chest and head voices easily. This song starts in a declamatory style, meaning that the vocal line is closer to speech than a lyrical phrase. The opening begins with a comfortable range and motion. The range for the entire song is B♭3–D4. As the song builds, it allows the young voice to use a beautiful head mix register. In addition to the melodic texture and register shifts, this piece requires excellent storytelling ability, and some singers may even want to add to the drama by

adding a British dialect. If the boy's voice starts dropping, it is always advisable to transpose, as this song is generally for an unchanged treble voice.

- **Born to Entertain** (Hal Leonard: *Kids' Musical Theatre Collection*)
For the growing female singer who is advanced in technique and stage presence, this song offers lots of complexity vocally, dramatically, and musically. When a young singer has a secure technique and stamina, with belting and mixing strategies, this song is a great adventure to learn and perform. Balancing the registers is demanding and requires a sophisticated young singer to manage it skillfully. The fragmented melody and harmonic structure need perceptive musicianship skills. The many syncopated rhythms, accents, triplets, and accidentals bring this sassy song to life. In addition to the musical elements, it demands the performer to be strong in dramatic interpretation. This showstopper piece is ambitious and has a dynamite ending, a great goal for young growing singers who want to show off their performance skills.

- **Count on Me** (Bruno Mars, Ari Levine and Phillip Lawrence)
Depending on age, most young singers come to voice lessons wanting to sing their favorite pop-rock songs. Once proper technique is secure, and children have learned repertoire that suits the discovering, learning, and growing singers' needs, it is fair to offer contrast and foster cross-training. Often children sing contemporary styles trying to sound like they are way ahead of their years in vocal timbre. Many of the pop tunes young kids are familiar with are difficult to vocally navigate because of the range, phrasing, and sophisticated register balancing. While some young singers might already have these advanced capabilities in place, most do not. As previously mentioned, children model the sounds they hear, which is not a healthy way for learning to sing at such a tender young stage of development. This song by Bruno Mars has a vocal range G3–C5 and has a rather straightforward melody. The register shifts are easy to navigate, and the stylization practices are fun to explore. Children should always perform these songs by maintaining the two training principles of intensity and duration.

SECTION IV
Teaching strategies for use in diversified settings

CHAPTER 16:
The Small Group Class

Working as a group fosters teamwork and a collective approach to skill building.

My first experiences working with children as a voice teacher were in large group classes. When I decided to begin teaching children, I was still under the impression that kids could not safely learn singing techniques in private lessons. I began teaching large groups thinking it was "safer." But somewhere along the line I asked myself, "What is the principle behind my teaching philosophy and why is it not suitable for children?" What I came to learn was far-reaching and beneficial, not only to the young singers, but to me personally and to my teaching strategies.

Group-class structuring is ideal for the beginning singer. Working as a group fosters teamwork and a collective approach to skill building. This structure can also be used as a monthly master-class, in addition to the private lesson, for independent students. Singing in groups has been recognized in various studies as a benefit to emotional and physical well-being. As mentioned previously, choral singing is not the only path to vocal fitness for children, and it certainly is not the only access to group singing. With group voice classes, children can work to gain confidence and discover their unique autonomous ability.

Providing voice classes in your local community creates an extraordinary possibility for a range of eager singers, serving a variety of needs. Not all children are interested in choral singing and others may not have access to a local children's choir. Some kids take band or other electives in school, but love singing and want to do both. While others are ready for one-on-one lesson structure, their parents might not be willing or able to afford private lessons. A group-class option is an opportunity for collaboration that meets the many needs of passionate singers. Introducing elemental skills in groups can be a perfect entry into the art of singing for many children, and they can experience it with a friend or sibling.

Group classes can be intimidating for a new teacher, but the *Five-Step System* is very adaptable and works in this setting. Weekly class times can last anywhere from 45 to 60 minutes, devoting half of the course to mind-body, breath, musicianship and vocalizing, and the other half to learning and performing fun solo songs.

Managing more than one singer can be a challenge or joy for the singing teacher. Some of the exercises in the *Five-Step System* will be need to be adjusted for small or large groups, and some classroom and group leadership skills are necessary for maintaining organization. While I modeled my group classes off of the concept of vocal master classes and adult group singing classes, I also used my years of classroom teaching to foster instructional objectives and classroom management. Preparation and lesson planning is the key to a successful group class.

An introductory course in the study of singing helps children who are not ready to work in a solo lesson setting. Working with a small group class can ease them slowly into the notion of singing alone, especially if they are shy or just starting out. They can find a more natural path to singing without the focus and attention directly on them as an individual. In a small group from two to six singers, they can feel like they are part of an elite clan and find commonality with other kids who share their passion. Solo study can often feel isolating, while working in groups encourages teamwork and fellowship. It is best if the teacher can keep age groups and ability levels together. Sometimes it can be a challenge to fill a small group with the same level, but it is possible with minor adjustments and attention to individual needs.

Offer the groups as a weekly class for six, ten, or twelve-week semesters. This structure gives the teacher a chance to have a course objective and decide what each group should be able to demonstrate after the completion of each semester. Flesh out a syllabus and have direction with goals for the class. Consider what skills should be understood and mastered, how many songs they should learn, and what the overall desired outcome is for the session. Each weekly class should also have a prepared lesson plan to keep order and cohesion. Below is a breakdown of the *Five-Step System* adapted for small group classes with suggestions for integration.

Most of the students taking group classes are in the *Discover Your Voice* category. Many of the same exercises apply as laid out in the previous chapters. Some tips and tricks to keep in mind, when working with groups, are explained here for easy reference.

1. **Mind and Body Warm-Ups:** Start the first class with a warm-up that introduces each singer to the others. The primary objective is to get to know one another. Set an intention for the class to focus on the teacher and learn how to listen musically. Kids in small groups can get overly friendly with each other, which is fun, but can also be distracting if they get too chatty and disorderly. Drawing them into active listening and observing is the main objective.

   - **Introduction:** Who Stole the Cookie
     - **Technique:** Learning how to introduce themselves, pay attention and keep a steady beat.
     - **Set-Up:** Sitting on the floor in a circle.
     - **Activity:** Chanting the motif: "Who stole the cookie from the cookie jar," with the response "[Name] stole the cookie from the cookie jar," etc. While sitting and tapping, the group not only learns each other's names, but they also work on listening, chanting, moving, and keeping a steady beat. The class is required to pay attention and focus.
     - **Tip:** Before the exercise, go around the circle and have each singer, stand up, and introduce themselves. Once the class progresses beyond the first few weeks, use this exercise to change tempos.

   - **Lying Down or Sitting:** Guided Meditation
     - **Technique:** Self-awareness. Improves concentration and relieves anxiety.
     - **Set-up:** Have them lie still on their backs, with eyes closed, and with their feet meeting in the middle of a circle fanning out like a blossom. Alternately, have the class sit in a circle, achieving a tall, seated position.
     - **Activity:** Have the group experience calmness by bringing their attention inward. As a guided meditation,

ask the class to squeeze their right fist. While holding the tension, take two deep breaths. Then relax and feel the tension release. Continue exercise with the other hand and then to the feet.

- **Tip:** Introduce this exercise once the class progresses, and the participants are familiar with one another. Children in a group class have a hard time closing their eyes. There will be a lot of excitement and activity. Guide them to a place where they can feel relaxed and unwind.

What *Group Singers* should know from this step: The objective should be to keep order and focus while keeping the fun and sociability of the group class. Help them to relax and connect with their internal sensations.

2. **Breathing and Posture Exercises:** These exercises can be done efficiently in a group. Pair them as a team-building exercise. When standing, have the singers work with a partner, observing together, and offering joint feedback.

- **Stretching:** Movement
  - **Technique:** Get the body moving while bringing awareness to lengthening the spine.
  - **Set-up:** Stand tall.
  - **Activity:** Pretend to be Jack and the Beanstalk and climb up to the sky.
  - **Tip:** Use this exercise to stand up and get moving after the sitting exercises. To keep the kids from getting out of control, advise them to hold space between each other, keeping their feet planted on the floor, so they stay in one place.

- **Vertical Breath:** Standing
  - **Technique:** Breath motion and body awareness.
  - **Set-up:** Stand tall.
  - **Activity:** Instruct the class to take a deep breath. Young singers typically overemphasize this motion. Use it as an opportunity to bring their attention to breathing low, without the shoulders rising. Pair them with a buddy and ask them to observe each other breathing without lifting the shoulders. Have them work together, taking turns, with one student watching and one student demonstrating.
  - **Tip:** Direct the students to touch their own shoulders as they breathe, observing the tendency to create tension.

- **Horizontal Breath:** Lay on the floor with feet in the middle of a circle creating a space of unity.
  - **Technique:** Experience correct inhalation and exhalation motion.
  - **Set-up:** Lie down on the back.
  - **Activity:** Have them place their hands on their bellies and inhale, feeling breath motion rising on inhale and lowering on exhale.
  - **Tip:** Try getting the group to close their eyes and direct their attention inward.

What *Group Singers* should know from this step: As with singers studying privately, voice class students should begin to understand the concepts of breath motion and stability. Singers should know the proper poise and posture required for singing.

3. **Musicianship:** Small group classes can easily use a workbook series together, or the teacher can design a curriculum of essential theory and aural skills based around introducing the solfege system, rhythm and basic notation. With large group classes, using a workbook can be a bit more challenging if the children are at different stages of maturity and musicianship. Below are a few suggestions for group games and activities related to musicianship skills.

- **Beat Motion:** Rhythm Passing Game
  - **Technique:** Learning to hear and feel the beat motion.
  - **Set-Up:** Sitting on the floor.
  - **Activity:** Singing the song "I Pass the Shoe" while passing their shoes around in the circle.
  - **Tip:** Have each student use one of their shoes. Get them to move, as a group, with the beat while singing. Use a metronome and change the tempo.

- **Pitch Matching:** Echo Songs
  - **Technique:** Echo and call-and-response songs are practical group activities because they cover several skills at once, listening, following, pitch matching, and the opportunity to randomly select singers to sing independently with a response.
  - **Set-up:** Standing
  - **Activity:** Singing an echo song like "No More Pie" or "My Aunt Came Back" (Appendix, pp. 122, 124).
  - **Tip:** Start this song by having the group echo in unison. As they gradually gain confidence, point out an individual recipient to be the echo.

- **Other suggested activities for group musicianship building:**
  - **Solfege:** Introduce Curwen/Kodaly hand signs.
  - **Vocal Exploration:** Ascending and descending motion.
  - **Notation:** Learn the staff and how to follow a musical score.
  - **Harmony:** As the small group advances in aural skills and depending on the age and ability of each class, introduce singing in rounds.

What *Group Singers* should know from this step: Listening, pitch matching, movement with the beat, and the ability to identify ascending and descending motion. Integrate an introduction to note reading skills.

4. **Vocal Technique:** Fundamental singing skills can systematically be addressed in voice class and should be consistently reviewed and promoted. Start the vocal exercises by having the students sing together. Throughout the examples, have singers take turns executing parts of the repeated sequence. I call this the *Stand-Out-Singer Approach*. This approach gives the teacher a chance to determine where each child is at vocally and allows for personal feedback and awareness. Establish independent singing and the ability to accept feedback from the teacher. Below is a recap of the recommended vocal exercise sequence. Begin vocal warm-ups with light head voice singing, followed by chest and speaking voice ranges, ending with light, flexible singing. Before introducing group classes to fuller chest and belt voice singing, it is in the best interest to establish a secure head voice register. To keep balance, kids need to develop light singing before fuller singing.
   - **Vocal Exploration:** Head and chest voice awareness
   - **Vocal Glides:** Ascending and descending motion
   - **Vocalization with Pitches:** Singing exercises in head and chest voice
   - **Diction:** Articulation, and projection
   - **Mix:** Finding the brightness
   - **Expression:** Singing with emotion
   - **Scales:** Singing with a range of motion using a light head voice

What *Group Singers* should know from this step: The four fundamental topics should include an understanding of registers, articulation, posture, and expression.

5. **Repertoire:** Private voice lessons and group classes follow the same structure, but one of the most significant differences in a voice class is the choice and execution of repertoire. It is most effective and convenient to manage when the whole group purchases the same songbook and learns the selected songs together. All of the singers can perform the assigned solo songs collectively as a class and as soloists. At the end of the session, each participant will have the ability to choose their favorite song to refine as a solo, for a final showcase performance. Using a collection that offers soundtracks featuring children soloists and additional accompaniment tracks serve as a practice tool at home. Having samples of children singing with age-appropriate technique is helpful for independent home study. Assigning songs eliminates the discussion about what songs they would like to sing. The fewer options a group has, the more amenable they become. When they all learn the same songs, they can decide from the compiled collection which one is their favorite and is most suitable to their voice. The added benefit to this is that they all learn several songs and gain a varied assortment of repertoire.

Teaching songs to a group class should be efficient and fun. Start by playing or singing the song. Integrate a rote learning style for mastering new songs. Introduce a new song each week working in class and at home. Assign many listening examples to enhance the learning process. The listening assignments should include children singing, so the students have age-appropriate models. It is also helpful to offer equal-level singers as listening examples. Create YouTube playlists to share with the class highlighting children and other performances of the song. It's OK if the performance isn't exactly the same arrangement, and may have alterations in pitch and rhythm; these can be opportunities for young singers to hear a different version. A variety of samples can support learning and listening skills.

Based on the ages and level of the group, follow the guidelines in the *Discover, Learn, and Grow Curriculum* for picking songs and learning repertoire. Here are some of the enhanced activities a group can enjoy when learning and mastering songs:

- Play games with expression by using expression cards. Using an assortment of index cards with examples of different emotions (happy, sad, funny, angry, etc.) have a volunteer choose one from the deck, have them sing the song using the expression found on the card. Keep the expressions simple.

- Invite students to volunteer and speak the text with expression for the class.

- The Mini Master Class (See below)

The Mini Master Class: One of my favorite aspects of working with a group is the ability to engage children in a growth mindset, to help them overcome the fear of failure and create resiliency. Teaching singers to give and receive feedback is a valuable singing skill. Each meeting should incorporate opportunities for participants to sing out. Once the class has learned their repertoire, spend the last ten minutes of every class asking for volunteers to come up and perform. Each singer should learn how to introduce themselves and their song to the audience. The introduction helps encourage poise, projection, and empowerment.

In many cases, there may be a shy or timid singer who would prefer to perform with someone else. Partners and small trios can sing together. Gradually allow the singers to gain confidence, and as they do, motivate them to perform a short phrase of the song alone, alternating verses with their partners. These small steps toward independence serve as supportive and progressive cultivation in the mastery of performance skills.

Following an in-class performance, the instructor should invite the student audience to share feedback on the performance. The highlights should focus on the skills that they have learned. Give the class some suggestions to help them understand the skill set they are learning and reinforce the techniques learned. A general rule for the class, when offering and accepting feedback, is that the kids should always provide at least two strengths about the performance and one opportunity for growth, making this a lesson about singing fueled by courage and empathy.

What *Group Singers* should know from this step: Performance practices. In every group session, the teacher should have an objective or end goal for what skills and techniques the class should achieve. Usually, that goal is to perform a solo song, duo, group song with a solo line, or recite a poem for an invited audience.

CHAPTER 17:
Large Group Classes

Confidence can grow when they share with their peers.

Working with a larger group of kids—about 7–15 participants—has an entirely different feel and flow than the intimate small group class. There are many advantages of large group classes for both teacher and young singers. Offering more singing opportunities to a broader range of students can help advertise a teacher's studio by bringing more exposure in the local region. Large group singing classes provide a favorable connection for parents, teacher, students, and community. Once the teacher has decided to add large group classes to their teaching schedule, it is necessary to plan well in order to host a successful class.

First, if your current space will not accommodate a large group, you must locate a suitable space near the current studio locale, like a classroom or choir room. There should be a piano, with plenty of room to move around and an area for highlighting solo performances. Consider offering large group classes through community centers, worship centers like churches and temples, or public or private local schools. Reach out to these different organizations and see what might fit your large group needs.

Advertising the class is also a consideration. Spread the word in as many places as possible to fill the voice class with eager and excited singers. The local community centers and enrichment programs are opportune locations to host the weekly sessions, since they often manage the advertising and can help offset the costs for the teacher trying to promote the classes on their own.

Group classes are generally offered after school, in the late afternoon, or as an early evening enrichment activity. These courses could also serve the homeschool cohort during the daytime hours, although many homeschool groups usually work on a co-op basis. When working with younger children, the group classes should be scheduled with enough time to unwind after school and grab a snack. They should not be scheduled too late, when it can interfere with bedtime routines. Generally speaking, the best time for afterschool class is between 4:30–6:30 pm.

The large group allows children to integrate into solo singing slowly. Many timid singers would prefer to only sing in the shower! Many come to a group class hoping to blend in and not stand out, often because they are terrified by the thought of singing for others. But these children love to sing and have a song in their heart. In a large class, the budding performer can explore the many facets of singing solo techniques without having to be showcased or standout. In my experience, nearly every child gains enough confidence to perform a solo song, single phrase within a song, or in some cases, to recite a poem for the audience. Any one of these moments is a huge accomplishment and especially empowering for shy and timid children.

Large classes bring benefits for the teacher as well. The ability to reach more children through the gift of song can be fun and quite energizing, and the environment can create a lot of sociability and merriment. Teachers can gain many new insights on how children learn and how to execute vocal techniques. The costs for participants can also be an asset; when offering a lower rate for a higher volume of singers, the teacher can yield a higher revenue for their time. Creating more income resources by adding more price points for the independent teacher makes good business sense.

The big bonus for group-class learning is the opportunity children have in observing one another. Kids do not spend enough time hearing other kids sing. In group-class, children become better listeners by inspiring community and friendship through singing. They hear more examples of age-appropriate singing, which is typically lacking in their understanding of good vocal practices. As I have pointed out, children often have misconceptions about what good singing is because they mostly model their sounds from adult professional singers. Confidence can grow when they share with their peers. While a shy singer often prefers group-class singing to private lessons, it is often this same singer who develops courage and becomes successful at performing for the group.

I had a student named Hunter who experienced tremendous stage fright. He didn't present as a shy personality; in fact he was quite expressive and outspoken in class. He was extremely bright, had a lovely voice, and offered terrific contributions in the group sharing. But he was terrified to sing alone. Gradually, Hunter developed confidence by performing with a partner, speaking the texts aloud, and taking small steps to increase his desire to function as a soloist. He attended several group-class semesters and went on to compete with a solo in a local festival. Hunter even performed on a large outdoor stage at a community event, where a massive audience commended his performing and singing ability. Hunter's achievement has proven that group classes can be a successful way to teach solo singing, while gently accentuating independence and confidence.

To avoid pitfalls, plan carefully. Classroom and behavior management can be handled by keeping the kids on task and focused while maintaining a good flow of fun teaching strategies and lesson planning.

Some of the pitfalls to consider:

- Variety or mismatch of ages and stages

- Different skill levels and abilities

- The need to work individually with a singer on a specific skill

- Space and location challenges

- Lesson flow and time management

- Attendance and late arrivals

- Behavior management with a group assembly

As mentioned, most group-class singers are beginners and are in the category of *Discover Your Voice*, no matter the age. It is possible to get an advanced student in a small or large group class, in which case they might be advised to pursue private lessons after an initial group session. In the case that not all kids in the class are at the same level, there are several ways to adjust and allow for a variety of ages and stages. For example, an advanced student in a group class can become a leader and helper if managed correctly. There are many ways to keep students engaged and inspired, no matter their ability. Enlist the more advanced students to be helpers and assign them extra challenges for at-home practice.

Working with children who need a little extra help on specific singing skills can also be a common problem. Children routinely struggle to access the head voice. It can be more challenging in a group setting to help a child who is struggling with finding a lighter vocal sound. It is essential not to single out a student in a negative way or to make a child feel like they are not succeeding at a particular skill. If it is clear that a singer is struggling to sing in the correct register, or any other technique, work with the whole group to nurture that specific tactic. Utilizing echo songs can serve the purpose of hearing a child sing independently. When inviting the group to echo, alternate individual recipients for the

> **BONUS TIP:**
> *Always try to limit the vocal range and only pick out the easiest of exercises to sing out independently. It is not a good idea to ask a timid singer to sing something challenging. Gently nurture through easy and accessible examples.*

response. When all singers are encouraged to sing out by themselves, they will gain more confidence as a whole instead of being singled out for a mistake. This strategy will also be useful during vocalization exercises. Ask for volunteers, rotate, or choose one person to sing alone. In an instance that a shy singer is not ready to sing out independently, never force them. Hopefully, in time, they will gain confidence. In some situations, the teacher might offer to have a singer stay after or come a little early to class for some one on one work and share some simple strategies. The joy of this style of teaching is watching the young singers bloom and grow.

To achieve efficient lesson flow and time management in large groups, follow the *Five-Step System*. Below are some suggestions for implementing changes in the curriculum.

Five-Step System Large Group Adaptations:

Mind and Body Warm-Ups: As with the smaller classes, the initial warm-ups can be offered in large groups for introductions, and as a way for children to ground themselves into the learning process for the day's activities. Start each class by sitting in a circle. The main idea for mindfulness is the same as it is for individuals and small groups: get the singers focused on the teacher and thinking about singing and musical concepts. Get the activity started as soon as the class begins. Keeping the group busy on an exercise will divert their energy to the task and not to socializing with each other. With large group classes, the warm-up session most likely will be interrupted by children arriving late, so keep space for the late arrivers and invite them to slip into the circle and join the activity quietly.

Breathing and Posture Exercises: In the large group classes, mixing and matching activities in the sequence should be executed with the least amount of transition from one to the other. For time and classroom management, these exercises should be brief and straightforward. The main idea is laying the foundation for proper breath and directing the notion of poise. This step can be a simple stretch as an awareness-building skill. Use props, like the pinwheel and straw, which are always fun. Be careful of over-excitement and unnecessary distractions, and only use props in a way that is functional and supported by well-planned lessons.

Musicianship: Aural skills are the main focus in big classes. Introduce the Curwen/Kodaly hand signs, using large flashcards or visuals. Echo songs are beneficial for evaluating individual singers, pitch-matching, and ear-training exercises. If the class is on the smaller side (ten or less) and is meeting for 12–15 weeks, notation and music-reading skills can be introduced. But for the sake of classroom management, the concentration should be on listening and performing.

Vocalizing: Following the guidelines described in the small group classes for vocal warm-ups, the large group will need a different setup. Depending on the size of the group and the location, the students will need to have chairs available. Set up the chairs in a single arched row around the piano, or, if in a choir room, straight rows on risers. It is best to face the students when they vocalize. The teacher must be able to see all of the students' faces and posture while singing. If possible, have the class stand around the piano so the teacher can hear them more closely. If it is not possible to have them near the teacher, definitely make use of alternating individuals as independent singers. In the large group setting, it can be harder to designate solo singers without the feeling of being singled out. When appointing a single singer to perform a fragment, do not offer much feedback, except to cheer on their bravery. Make it a triumphant moment and an opportunity to sing independently. The teacher can also ask each singer, one by one, to perform a vocal sequence. Advocating for solo opportunities in small increments is advised. Establish a firm foundation in head voice singing and unleashing the freedom to let go and have fun.

Repertoire: The students' favorite part of the class will likely be learning and performing songs. The recommendations set forth in Chapter 11 regarding the choosing of repertoire will serve as a guide for success. Include in the syllabus some skills on how to be a good audience member. The Mini-Master Class format serves as a perfect opportunity for learning how to listen attentively and applaud each performance. The children will often get tired and wander off emotionally when others are singing, so encourage them to be active listeners and show the performer some recognition and feedback.

When learning the repertoire in the songbooks, it is recommended to supplement by adding in some folk songs and world music. For the older singers (ages 9–13), introduce them to rounds and new languages. "Dona Nobis Pacem" is a perfect introduction to singing in Latin. It can be performed in unison or as a round, while gradually building skills. "Shalom Chaverim" is another easy round to introduce kids to a variety of languages and culture. Teach the song each week by introducing small phrases. Classic American folk songs like "Home on The Range," "This Land is Your Land," or "She'll Be Comin' Round the Mountain" are a few other examples of Traditional Americana songs in unison that can also be sung in the group class. Investigate unique choices and expose your singers to uncommon and fun song literature, so that they can begin to understand more than just the immediate world around them. Broaden their young minds by adding a little history and culture to the repertoire part of the class.

By the end of the semester or session, students should be able to demonstrate a variety of appropriate singing skills. They should be able to walk on a stage (or performance space), show excellent poise, introduce themselves utilizing projection and articulation, and perform a song from memory, with accompaniment, while keeping a steady tempo. Singers should be using proper singing technique including a balance of registers, good diction, and expression. The students should also know how to take a bow and walk off stage. When young singers have accomplished these goals, the voice teacher will feel an immense sense of a "job well done."

CHAPTER 18:
Online Singing

Learning to sing using innovation gives students an opportunity to thrive.

Voice lessons don't always have to be offered face-to-face in the neighborhood studio setting. Many teachers offer their expertise exclusively online to reach a wider audience and clientele. No matter the delivery method, a systematic lesson structure has proven successful. For those who do teach in person, offering online lessons can serve as a substitute for the occasional weather disruption, life disruption, or when the teacher or student are out of town. Teachers who wish to expand their offerings, and develop new ways of delivering content, can explore modifications to in-person lesson structure.

The global pandemic caused by COVID-19 (beginning in late 2019) gave many teachers no other choice but to remodel their lesson delivery and move their studios to an online format. Because of the Five-Step System framework, I was able to easily offer continuity and consistency to my students. For teachers new to navigating online technology, there can be some logistical challenges. But for those teachers who work with a systematic curriculum, there will be no interruptions regarding content and objectives for private lessons or group classes. By making minor adjustments for remote learning, both teacher and student can continue to benefit from a structured lesson curriculum.

Besides the convenience of anytime and anywhere, here are some of the benefits of internet-based voice lessons:

- The voice teacher gains new visual perspectives when observing posture, alignment, and expression

- The teacher and student must listen to each other with more attention to detail and consideration

- The student must become aurally independent by not relying on piano accompaniment to support every note

- The teacher has the opportunity to create fresh and innovative strategies

- The student can see themselves on the screen, which fosters a better perception of how they implement a skill or technique

- Video conferencing platforms with screen-sharing capabilities allow teachers and students to interact by using more online resources

Being armed with specific knowledge about the developmental ages and stages can be beneficial when facilitating an online environment. Working with a twelve-year-old online is entirely different than working with a five-year-old. Many of the same principles for face-to-face lessons can be reinforced online. Any child who is normally observed by a parent or caregiver in an in-person lesson should be supported at home in the same manner for an online voice lesson. Having an adult present on the other end for younger students is a must, both for taking notes and managing technology. Even the older students in the tween years may need some adult support and guidance when managing sound adjustments and electronic components within the online meeting platforms.

The biggest challenge when working online is the lack of synchronization. Light travels faster than sound. Therefore, there are delays when attempting to have a unity of sound. This lag time creates challenges for accompanying your singers and singing or playing in real-time with the student. This can be mitigated by the singer using accompaniment tracks on their end of the stream, which must be played from a separate device from the one live-streaming the lesson.

It is essential to set clear boundaries with children when working online, and these boundaries will have a different context than in the studio. If a student has previously worked with the teacher in person, understand that learning in a new environment can be challenging for children who are used to a routine. Try to keep as much semblance of normality as possible. Just like in-person lessons, it is crucial to create smooth transitions from one step to the next when teaching lessons online. This is especially true for *Discover Your Voice Singers*, who can often lose their attention much faster. Online lessons require more preparation outside of the lesson to assure organization and efficiency.

If the teacher is leading small or large group classes online, many features in the various meeting platforms can offer assistance. There are mute buttons and hand-raising features, which help to create structure and class management. Since the student is at home, it is essential to have them set up a personalized workspace for carrying out their lesson activities. Bedrooms can often cause distractions and are a bit too private and personal to serve as suitable studio space (and could also pose an issue regarding child protection and safety). A working studio environment with children is best in an open space with room to move and good lighting (avoid backlighting and over-head glares). Remember always to keep it playful, engaging, and intentional.

Ages and Stages: Adjustments for Online Teaching
Discover Your Voice (ages 5–7):

1. **Mind and Body Warm-Ups:** The goal is to instill participation with focus and independent responsiveness. It can be helpful to start the lesson in a child-sized chair and work on stretches and movement from a grounded spot. This position allows the teacher to start the lesson by interacting face-to-face and targeting the one-on-one collaboration. The online setting naturally puts the teacher and student on the same level and allows for good eye contact. The teacher should make every attempt to look into the eye of the camera lens to assure that they are looking straight at the student. Once the child is following directions well and is focused, the teacher can begin to offer standing exercises that stay well within the viewing window.

   Allowing for movement and flexibility is helpful for wiggly young singers, and lots of activities can happen while sitting. From this grounded position it is easy to explore echo songs and call-and-response activities, which encourage focus and collaboration. Echo songs can be fun and effective to add in actions and gestures, and animated movements can help the singer with expression. The parent should be sitting close by, taking notes, and participating as an active listener, only offering support as needed for logistics.

2. **Breathing and Posture:** These exercises and strategies can flow right out of the first step while the child is still sitting, reminding them of the length and tall spine that they created in their body warm-ups. If the student has a pinwheel or other props at home for breath awareness, they can use these devices as the teacher continues to develop a knowledge of breath motion. If students don't have props at home, the teacher can still use creative ways to instill imagination and play, utilizing the props as visual aids.

3. **Musicianship:** If the teacher is using meeting platforms that offer share-screen compatibility, it is best to explore note-reading when the student is still sitting with good posture in a chair. Using a whiteboard, it is also easy to draw and share vocal expression lines for discovering pitch motion of ascending and descending patterns. Continue with teaching solfege hand signs and echo songs for pitch matching skills. The Full Voice curriculum offers many online resources for remote learning, which can be lots of fun.

4. **Vocalizing:** Invite the student to remove their chair and stand for this portion of the lesson, reminding them to keep length in their spine and shoulders away from ears. Exploring vocal warm-ups without the capability of accompanying the singer requires a slower pace and more attention on listening and feeling the sensations. Teachers can have singers add in body percussion and rhythmic responses to help keep attention. It is best to start with less range of motion in pitch sequencing as the singer adapts to singing unaccompanied. Vocal glides and head voice singing should still be the main point of development. Explore articulation exercises through tongue twisters and chest voice awareness.

5. **Repertoire:** The singer can perform their songs with the piano accompaniment tracks. Teaching new songs to Discovery Singers can be coached using creative ideas by echoing short phrases and preparing listening examples outside of the lesson. Incorporating audiation and the ability to "think-sing" is also a skill that can be reinforced with online teaching. Beyond singing and performing fun songs, the Discovery Singer begins to cultivate expression and articulation through fun strategies and playful exercises.

Learn Your Voice (ages 8–10)

1. **Mind and Body Warm-Ups:** Start in a seated position where the child is grounded and sitting with their feet firmly planted on the ground. Go through a series of fun and intentional exercises for lengthening the neck and spine. As the singer learns more about their singing voice, guide them in bringing their attention inward, and foster an ability to feel sensations and avoid distractions. Begin the online voice lesson with meditation and listening exercises. Invite the singer to close their eyes and go on a listening scavenger hunt. Guide them to calm down their sensory reactions and in silence, pick three different things they can hear in their house. Then ask them to tell you what they heard. After they become aware of their surroundings and enter into focused attention, they are ready to begin their lesson with purpose.

2. **Breathing and Posture:** In the seated position, invite the singer to breathe slowly into their nose as if they were smelling a rose, exhaling through the nose, feeling the motion of breath coming in and out. From this upright seated position, the singer can explore using the strategies and props (if they have them) like the blow-ball for stability and regulation of breath flow management. It is still easy to incorporate accessories, especially if the singer has their own at home. If not, the teacher can use them as an example to generate the physical reaction using mental awareness and imagery.

3. **Musicianship:** The student can work on a variety of musicianship skills. Mastering the solfege scale (both ascending and descending) and learning note and rhythm values can be easy and fun online by using screen-sharing and/or other apps and websites available for theory and aural skills training.

4. **Vocalizing:** Modifying vocal exercises for online teaching requires an even more deliberate approach and should continue to address the skill-building sequence for singers learning to navigate through different styles and techniques. Teachers can prepare recordings of vocalises and send them to the student before the lesson. In this way, students can use the tracks to accompany themselves and sing along. An alternative would be for the teacher to play block chords, encouraging the ability to sing a cappella and assisting the singer with correct pitches and stability. This method works best if the teacher has a good microphone and strong internet connection.

5. **Repertoire:** Utilizing creativity and a variety of strategies for learning and executing songs, the students can not only perform their songs with accompaniment tracks, but they can also spend time cultivating their skill advancement in expressive singing and performing. At this level, songs can also be taught through echoing of phrases, making sure to correct the notes with deliberate attention, and the singer can work to

become more independent by learning the song on their own. It can be fun and inspiring to host online group sessions for the singers to sing for one another if they aren't already in a group class setting.

Grow Your Voice (ages 11–13)

1. **Mind and Body Warm-Ups:** With singers of all ages, the lesson should start with guided meditation appropriate for each age and stage of development. For older children, a great place to start is a recap of the skills and observations the singer has made since the previous lesson. Practicing independence and establishing a good work ethic are skills they should be cultivating. The guided meditation exercises in Chapter 15 are easy to employ in the online setting. The tween-aged singer is most likely already well-acquainted with using media for interacting and socializing.

2. **Breathing and Posture:** Either sitting or standing, the students can easily develop the skills for stability and control of breath flow management.

3. **Musicianship:** Most students in this age group are independent and accustomed to technology; they can enjoy a wide variance of online learning methods. Allow creativity to guide their developing musical skills. If they have an interest in learning an instrument, like the ukulele, help them find online tutorials. Various websites and YouTube videos offer resources for learning how to harmonize, sight-read, and even how to riff. Explore these internet-based applications and continue building a foundation of musical training in a variety of ways.

4. **Vocalizing:** Vocalizing with more range of motion and utilizing a variety of genres requires the teacher to listen with more focus in online lessons. To make the adjustments for desired resonance and tone quality, the student and teacher will vocalize at a slower pace, applying attention to details. Through this pacing, quality will surpass quantity. Allow the motion to be more discerning for making corrections and suggestions. As the young singer develops the skills to feel subtle changes, this pace will serve the student well in developing a good foundation in singing technique.

5. **Repertoire:** The growing singer should be developing independence when learning their songs, and can employ all of the same guidelines in face-to-face lessons as they do in the online platform. Sharing online videos and other resources makes collaborating fun. However, the teacher may spend more time outside of the lesson, preparing resources.

Online Performing:

Making recordings of singers is another way to diversify teaching and performing strategies. In the modern digital world, it is common and easy to create quality videos at home and in the studio. Many young singers are already making videos for fun on social media websites. It is easy to guide students in creating a refined video that highlights the skills and talents they are learning in their lessons, and it is becoming essential in the performing industry. There are several opportunities for video submissions for young singers, including online auditions and competitions, and virtual studio recitals. Performances can be delivered as a live event, or a pre-recorded video can be uploaded to various media platforms for viewing.

It is essential to remind the singer that proper singing technique still comes first. But because video gives us a visual as well, it is necessary to share the key mechanics of curating a quality result. Having some technology and recording savvy is helpful but not required. It is easy to secure a distinctive video by just using a smartphone or other hand-held media device. The quality of the video lies in the setup. Topics for consideration include camera angles, where to look when performing for a camera, what to wear, designing the best sound balance and acoustics, what is in the background, and lighting; all of these aspects contribute to a refined and satisfactory performance. Younger singers or those inexperienced with the recording device will need a trusted adult to help in producing the video, and laying out some guidelines will help.

Camera Angles: The camera should be facing the singer. I prefer the camera recording at eye level, but considerations can be made to film from below or above as well. A head-on frontal view helps the audience engage more with the performer. It is best to shoot in a horizontal orientation, as it will naturally fit screens of all sizes and facilitate editing. When recording videos for virtual ensembles, it is essential to have continuity in the camera orientation, so that singers appear uniform in the virtual grid. Recording with a horizontal angle is best for groups, so there is no space between the videos on the screen.

Where to Look: Many young singers find it challenging to focus their attention during a performance and struggle to direct their gaze. Often their eyes will wander all over the place. It is not always necessary to look directly at the camera, but children can benefit from a focal point, which should be in the direction of the camera. Singers should create a scene in their minds and conceive the ambiance of being on a stage, pretending the camera is an audience member.

Appearance: The singer should make wardrobe considerations based on the type of mood or character they are hoping to convey and dress in a way that reflects this in their performance. In most cases, the audience or reviewer of the video wants to see at least three quarters of the body or the full body. In most virtual choir videos, a headshot is enough to get more focus on the individual where it will be featured among a collage of other performers. Take this into consideration when choosing what to wear, so that the entire outfit suits the performance and personality.

Sound Balance and Acoustics: When recording at home, the singer should test to find out if they get a better sound when window treatments are closed. Some open spaces will achieve more echo, while other areas that have lots of upholstery, carpeting, and heavy curtains will result in a drier sound. If the acoustics of the home are unsatisfactory, some churches and large open spaces can provide excellent locations for obtaining good sound production. Perform sound checks by making short video snippets and listening back to determine if anything needs to be changed or altered. Using external microphones will improve sound quality, and using live accompaniments may also result in better sound. Make sure the piano is not too loud in the sound mix. If the singer uses an accompaniment track, the sound quality and balance should be tested before recording.

Background: Be aware of what is in the staged viewing area. The main focus should be on the singer, and distracting background scenery can pull the focus away from the performance. Some singers may choose to use a virtual background.

Lighting: Since most performance videos are taken inside, it is important to achieve good lighting to create a crisp and polished look. Allow natural light to enter the space, but do not let the natural light serve as a background light. It is best to have the light coming from in front of the subject. If the light is coming from the side, it will cast shadows on the face. A singer's countenance is their most valuable aspect of expressive performance, and it should be illuminated as best as possible. When recording during the evening hours, the same standards apply, and using lamps in front of the singer will create the most favorable lighting.

Make considerations for the type of video submission the student is producing. There will be different expectations for recitals, virtual choirs, auditions, and competitions. Before they begin the recorded performance, a singer may choose to use an introduction or slate to announce their name and what they will be performing (unless instructed by a competition not to do so). Although it is often hard to create that "one perfect performance," it is always good practice for the singer to realize that little mistakes are just a part of the process. Perfection is not the objective; the ultimate goal is a meaningful and captivating performance.

When working together on videos, teachers and students both gain valuable insight into performance aspects and can discuss strategies for improvement. The process also serves as objective support for singers who may have a habit of being overly critical when seeing and hearing themselves perform.

There are other logistics to consider when producing online videos with children. Before posting any video or photos of a student on the internet, a voice teacher must make sure to have secured the permission from parents or legal guardians to share the student's images and content. Unlike live performances, videos submitted online can potentially remain there for many years. Young singers will progress rapidly in their skills and age, and some children can become disenchanted with videos that were posted in their younger years. If the teacher is posting video content through their studio, they should consider what platforms they are using, making sure that they can take down a video at the request of the singer and their family.

While I find the face-to-face lesson scenario to be the best fit for my studio and teaching style with children, I gain tremendous knowledge when I allow innovation to guide new practices. There are a lot of creative ways to design the best suitable teaching platform for individual teaching studios. As technology and lifestyles change, there will always be a need for new delivery methods. Teachers and students can make great discoveries by adapting strategies for internet learning when times necessitate remote voice lessons. When working with children, the key to success remains in the content and understanding of teaching methods the instructor provides. By paying attention to developmental progress and using a five-step system, the teacher has more direction and purpose in cultivating success. In our ever-changing world, there are so many beautiful ways to discover, learn, and grow. Explore your toolbox, whether teaching online or in-person, for strategies that foster intentional growth and development while being innovative, flexible, and fun.

CODA

Planting the seeds of empowerment.

Empowering children to find their voices and accomplish artistic singing goals can be inspiring and very rewarding. It's hard for me to imagine that there was once a time when I passed up the opportunity to be a part of this work. I now know it was only due to a lack of understanding and knowledge. This realization makes me vow to bring even more awareness to this important aspect of vocal pedagogy.

I hope these pages have helped to formulate new teaching ideologies for working with all age groups. And I hope you are feeling equipped to welcome young children into your studio and maybe even consider teaching small and large group classes in your community. There are many rewards to teaching through these amazing years of a child's transformation. I have watched firsthand how once little kindergarteners with sweet, timid voices have blossomed into confident pre-teens and beyond in the voice studio. Celebrating these milestones of maturation is both fun to watch and wondrous. To be such an integral part of a child's development is enchanting.

Through my many years of teaching, I have worked with a variety of ages. In addition to working with children, I teach teens through the college years and have had many avocational adults in their retirement years come to study singing with me. Each stage of life brings a unique set of joys and enlightenment for the student. The childhood years, however, bring the most transformation and make the job for the private teacher even more extraordinary. It is gratifying to know you are planting seeds that will shape and formulate their musical experiences in the years to come, and it begins with a supportive environment and a curriculum designed for the child singer that evolves as they do.

Many of the strategies used for children are easily adaptable in lessons for all ages. Many adults suffer from not having enough "play" in their lives. Anyone can benefit from a comprehensive lesson system that offers the skills of mind and body focus, breath, and musicianship using props, imagination, and play, all while developing an efficient singing technique. When a student masters singing skills in a well-rounded curriculum, the results are evident in the beauty of their sound and their confidence in performance.

As the years evolve and our technology continues to advance, our teaching methods may change, but kids will still be kids with innocent curiosity and a love for play. Teaching singing to children must include creative interaction, with an ability to respond using tactile experiences, including props, movement, and imagination. I hope that teaching the art of singing using the methods contained in this book for pediatric pedagogy will enhance the world at large by instilling inspiration and confidence in those who learn from a young age. Here's to empowering singers of all ages, especially children, one lesson at a time.

BIBLIOGRAPHY

References:

Brunssen, K. (2018). *The Evolving Singing Voice: Changes Across the Lifespan*. Plural Publishing.

Cooksey, J. M. (1999). *Working with Adolescent Voices*. Concordia Publishing.

Feierabend, J.M. (2006). *First Steps in Music for Preschool and Beyond the Curriculum*. GIA Publications.

Harrison, S. D., & O'Bryan, J. (2014). *Teaching Singing in the 21st Century*. Springer.

Kahane, J C. (1982). *Growth of the Human Prepubertal and Pubertal Larynx*. Journal of Speech and Hearing Research, 25 (3): 446-55.

Loney, N. (2018*). Full Voice Teacher Guide Private and Small Group Voice Lessons for Singers 5-12 Years Old*. Full Voice Music.

McKinney, J.C. (2005). *The Diagnosis and Correction of Vocal Faults* (3rd ed). Waveland Press, Inc.

Phillips, K. H. (1996). *Teaching Kids to Sing*. Schirmer Books.

Saunders Barton, M., & Spivey, N. (2018). *Cross-Training in the Voice Studio: A Balancing Act*. Plural Publishing.

Saunders Barton, M. (2007). *Bel Canto Can Belto: Teaching women to sing musical theatre* [DVD tutorial]. Penn State Media Sales.

Saunders Barton, M. (2014). *Bel Canto Can Belto: What about the boys?* [DVD tutorial]. Penn State Media Sales.

Suzuki, D. S., & Suzuki, W. (1983). *Nurtured by Love: The Classic Approach to Talent Education*. Alfred Music.

Vennard, V. (1967). *Singing: The Mechanism and the Technic*. Carl Fischer.

Williams, J. (2013). *Teaching Singing to Children and Young Adults*. Compton Publishing.

Inspired Reading and Study:

Atterbury, B. (1984). *Children's Singing Voices: A Review of Selected Research*. Bulletin of the Council for Research in Music Education, (80), 51-63. Retrieved from http://www.jstor.org/stable/40317870

Baker Brehm, S., Kelchner, L.N., & Weinrich, B. D. (2014). *Pediatric Voice: A Modern, Collaborative Approach to Care*. Plural Publishing.

Blankenbehler, G., & Blankenbehler, E. (2012). *Singing Lessons for Little Singers: A 3-in-1 Voice, Ear-Training and Sight-Singing Method for Children*. CreateSpace Independent Publishing Platform.

Boytim, J. F. (2014). *The Private Voice Studio Handbook: A Practical Guide to All Aspects of Teaching* (Revised ed.). Hal Leonard Publications.

Brumfield, S. (2014). *First, We Sing! Kodály-Inspired Teaching for the Music Classroom*. Hal Leonard Publications.

Edwin, R. & Wilson Arboleda, B. (2008). *The Kid and the Singing Teacher* [DVD tutorial]. VoiceWise.

Furness, H. (2016, October 18). Royal Opera House to teach children to sing "healthily" over X Factor voice strain fears. *The Telegraph*. https://www.telegraph.co.uk/news/2016/10/18/royal-opera-house-to-teach-children-to-sing-healthily-over-x-fac/

Gackle, L. (2010). *Finding Ophelia's Voice, Opening Ophelia's Heart: Nurturing the Adolescent Female Voice: An Exploration of the Physiological, Psychological, and Musical Developments of Female Students.* Heritage Music Press.

Hartnick, C. J., & Boseley, M. E. (2010). *Clinical Management of Children's Voice Disorders*. Plural Publishing.

Healy, J. M. (2011). *Endangered Minds: Why Children Don't Think and What We Can Do About It.* Simon and Schuster.

Howard, D. M. (2014). "Ring" in the Solo Child Singing Voice. *Journal of Voice*, 28 (2), 161-169.

Howard, F. E. (1898). *The Child-Voice in Singing: Treated from a physiological and a practical standpoint, and especially adapted to schools and boy choirs* (New and rev. ed.). Novello, Ewer & Co.

Kagen, S. (1950). *On Studying Singing*. Dover Publications.

LeBorgne, W., & and Rosenberg, M. (2014). *The Vocal Athlete*. Plural Publishing.

Nhat Hanh, T. (2011). *Planting Seeds: Practice Mindfulness with Children*. Parallax Press.

Runfola, M., & Rutkowski, J. (2010). *TIPS: The Child Voice*. R&L Education.

Rutkowski, J. (1996). "The Effectiveness of Individual/Small-Group Singing Activities on Kindergartners' Use of Singing Voice and Developmental Music Aptitude." *Journal of Research in Music Education*, 44(4), 353–368. www.jstor.org/stable/3345447

Rutkowski, J., & Miller, M. S. (2002). *A Longitudinal Study of Elementary Children's Acquisition of Their Singing Voices*. Update: Applications of Research in Music Education, 22(1), 5–14. https://doi.org/10.1177/87551233020220010901

Skelton, K. D. (2007). The Child's Voice: A closer look at pedagogy and science. *Journal of Singing*, 63(5), 537-544.

Snel, E. (2013) *Sitting Still Like A Frog: Mindfulness Exercises for Kids (and Their Parents)*. Shambhala Publications.

Complete Hal Leonard Publications for Children

25 Folksongs for Children (HL00154679)

36 Solos for Young Singers (HL00740143)

36 More Solos for Young Singers (HL00230109)

Art Songs for Children (HL00211617)

The Boy's Changing Voice (HL00121394)

Boy's Songs from Musicals (HL00001127)

Broadway Presents! Kids' Musical Theatre Anthology (HL00322155)

Broadway Songs 4 Kids (Book only: HL00312076 | Book/Audio: HL00230103)

Children's Sacred Solos (HL00740297)

Christmas Solos for Kids (HL00740130)

Church Solos for Kids (HL00740080)

Daffodils, Violets & Snowflakes: High Voice (HL00740244)

Daffodils, Violets & Snowflakes: Low Voice (HL00740245)

Disney Collected Kids' Solos (HL00230066)

Disney Duets for Kids (HL00124472)

More Disney Solos for Kids (HL00740294)

Still More Disney Solos for Kids (HL00230032)

The Giant Book of Children's Vocal Solos (HL0053571)

Girls' Songs from 21st Century Musicals (HL00287561)

Girl's Songs from Musicals (HL00001126)

Kids' Broadway Songbook – Revised Edition (Book only: HL00311609 | Book/Audio: HL00740149 |
   Accompaniment CDs: HL00740316)

Kids' Holiday Solos (HL00740206)

Kids' Musical Theatre Audition: Girl's Edition (HL00001124)

Kids' Musical Theatre Audition: Boy's Edition (HL00001125)

Kids Sing Praise and Worship (HL00121351)

Kids' Songs from Contemporary Musicals (HL00129923)

Kids' Stage & Screen Songs (HL00740151)

Kids' Solo Vocal Collection (HL00119839)

Kids' Musical Theatre Collection, Volume 1 (HL00230029)

Kids' Musical Theatre Collection, Volume 2 (HL00230031)

(cont.)

Complete Hal Leonard Publications for Children (cont.)

Kids' Musical Theatre Collection, Volume 1 and 2 Complete (HL00124193)

Popular Solos for Young Singers (HL00740150)

Rodgers & Hammerstein Solos for Kids (HL00230030)

Sacred Vocal Solos for Kids (HL00110424)

The Singer's Musical Theatre Anthology: Children's Edition (Book only: HL00159518 | Book/Audio: HL00159519 | Accompaniment CDs: HL00159520)

Solos for Kids (HL00740021)

Solos from Musicals for Kids (HL00740079)

APPENDIX

IPA PRONUNCIATION GUIDE

SYMBOL	SAMPLE WORD
/i/ =	feet
/e/ =	egg
/a/ =	father
/o/ =	obey
/u/ =	pool
/æ/ =	cat
/ŋ/ =	hang
/ə/ =	sofa
/j/ =	yes

NEW STUDENT INTAKE FORM
Use this form for parents to share information about their child before lessons begin.

Please tell me about your child's musical experience: study, performance, participation in groups, singing at home, etc.

_____

_____

Please tell me about YOUR musical environment: any musicians or family members with a background in music in the home?

_____

_____

Do you listen to music in the home or car? If so, what kind of music do you enjoy listening to?

_____

_____

Do you have a piano at home?   Yes | No

What is your child's age, and has your child expressed interest to you in taking voice lessons?

_____

Does your child already like to sing? If so, what kind of music does your child enjoy singing?

_____

Is your child involved in other activities? If so, please list them.

_____

_____

Does your child have any special learning needs you would like me to know about?

_____

_____

Are you willing to advocate for your child's practicing in a supportive, positive way?   Yes | No

NEW STUDENT OBSERVATION AND FOLLOW-UP FORM

For ages 5–13 in the private studio

*This form is for the teacher's personal use, not to be given to the student.
Suggested use: At the first lesson, use this form to observe where the child is at developmentally, and then use it as a follow-up to check-in on progress each term.

Name _____ Age_____ Date_____

Mind and Body

Overall demeanor and poise__

Temperament(scared/nervous/distracted/focused/talkative/quiet) __

Attention span__

Parental interaction__

Respiration and Posture

Body Alignment__

Breath Coordination__

Musicianship

Ability to echo on same pitch__

Ability to read music__

Ability to keep a steady beat __

Vocal Technique

Speech sounds__

Volume level__

Head voice awareness__

Vocal range__

Quality of sound __

Repertoire

Style preference__

Previous experience__

Additional observations and comments:

Point Scale:

5	4	3	2	1
Already amazing!	Growth happening here!	Learning about this!	Beginning to discover!	Not quite yet

CHILD SINGER PERFORMANCE ASSESSMENT

Use this form for adjudication and assessment events
Ages 5–13

Name_____ Age_____ Date_____

POISE

Appearance and Temperament__

Slate__

Focus of Attention__

Confidence__

RESPIRATION AND POSTURE

Body Alignment__

Inhalation__

Stability of Breath__

Breath Phrasing__

MUSICIANSHIP

Correct notes and rhythms__

Balance and integration with accompaniment__

Dynamics__

VOCAL TECHNIQUE

Diction and articulation__

Register balancing__

Stability of tone__

Vowel resonance__

INTERPRETATION

Memorization__

Storytelling__

Facial expression__

Use of gestures__

Attention to style__

TOTAL POINTS

Point Scale:

5	4	3	2	1
Already amazing!	Growth happening here!	Learning about this!	Beginning to discover!	Not quite yet

MY SINGING PRACTICE CHART

	MONDAY	TUESDAY	WEDNESDAY	THURSDAY	FRIDAY	SATURDAY	SUNDAY
Warm-ups							
Respiration							
Ear Training/ Theory							
Vocalizing							
Repertoire							

Tongue Twisters and Articulation Exercises:

- Red leather, yellow leather (repeat 3x)

- Alyssa ate apples at the airport (repeat 3x)

- Karenna kept keys for King Kate (repeat 3x)

- Lovely Lady Laura ate long-length linguini

- Cate caught cool country cows

- Tick tock, tickety-tock (repeat 3x)

- Tip of the tongue and the teeth (repeat 3x)

- T-D-T-D-T-D-T-D-T

- Too hot, hot potato, potato pancake, pancake platter, platter scatter

- Nutter butter peanut butter

- Whether the weather be cold,
  Or whether the weather be hot,
  We'll be together whatever the weather
  Whether we like it or not

- Super singing Sally Sue
  Singing super silly songs
  All day long, to you

Songs and Activities

Wiggle Song
Tune: "For He's a Jolly Good Fellow"
My thumbs are starting to wiggle.
My thumbs are starting to wiggle.
My thumbs are starting to wiggle,
Around and around and around.

My hands are starting to wiggle.
My hands are starting to wiggle.
My hands are starting to wiggle,
Around and around and around.

Continue with other body parts.
Author: Unknown

Pass the Shoe

I pass the shoe from me to you, to you, I pass the shoe, and this is what I do.

I pass the shoe from me to you, to you
I pass the shoe, and this is what I do (2x)

(Repeat several times, changing tempo)

No More Pie

Echo Song

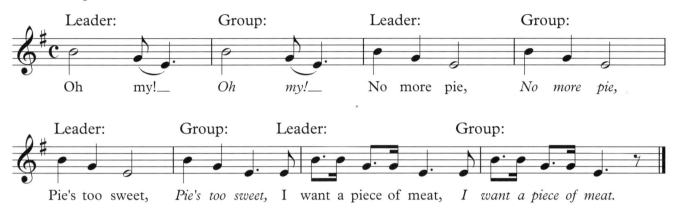

Oh, my! (echo)

No more pie, (echo)

Pie's too sweet, (echo)

I want a piece of meat (echo)

Meat's too red (echo)

I wanna piece of bread, (echo)

Bread's too brown, (echo)

I think I'll go to town, (echo)

Town's too far, (echo)

I think I'll take the car, (echo)

Car won't go, (echo)

I fell and stubbed my toe (echo)

Toe gives me pain, (echo)

I think I'll take the train, (echo)

Train had a wreck, (echo)

I fell and hurt my neck, (echo)

Oh, my! (echo)

No more pie. (echo)

Author: Unknown (Folk Song)

Chop, Chop, Chippity Chop
Action song with motions

Chop, chop, chippity chop
Cut off the bottoms and cut off the tops
What we have left, we will put in the pot
Chop, chop, chippity chop!

1. *Ask the student what they would like to make today (imaginary soup?)*

2. *Move hands in chopping motions*

3. *Scoop up imaginary veggies and put them in the pot*

Engine, Engine Number Nine
Action song with motions

Engine, Engine Number Nine
Going down Chicago Line
See it sparkle,
See it shine
Engine, Engine Number Nine

1. *Use percussion instruments (sand blocks or hands)*

2. *Move hands or sand blocks in a brushing motion*

Oh, My Aunt Came Back

Echo Song with motions

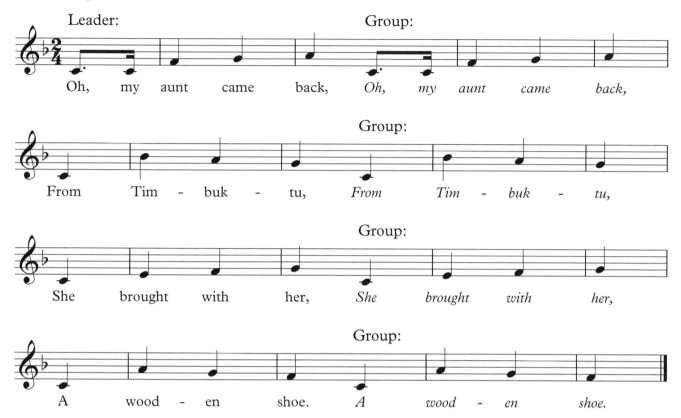

Oh, my aunt came back (Oh, my aunt came back)
From Timbuktu (From Timbuktu)
And brought with her (And brought with her)
A wooden shoe (A wooden shoe)
Start tapping one foot

Oh, my aunt came back (Oh, my aunt came back)
From old Japan (from old Japan)
And brought me back (And brought me back)
A waving fan. (A waving fan)
Start waving fan

Oh, my aunt came back (Oh, my aunt came back)
From old Algiers (From old Algiers)
And brought with her (And brought with her)
A pair of shears. (A pair of shears)
Use other hand and fingers miming scissors to snip

Oh, my aunt came back (Oh, my aunt came back)
from Guadeloupe (from Guadeloupe)
And brought with her (And brought with her)
A hula-hoop. (A hula-hoop)
Start swaying hips like a hula-hoop

Oh, my aunt came back (Oh, my aunt came back)
From the county fair (From the county fair)
And brought with her (And brought with her)
A rocking chair. (A rocking chair)
Rock back and forth

Oh my aunt came back (Oh, my aunt came back)
From the city zoo (From the city zoo)
And brought with her (And brought with her)
A nut like you! (A nut like you!)
Point to each other

Big Pig

Pitch Exploration Poem

"Where are you going Big Pig, Big Pig?"
  (Spoken in a light head voice)

"Out to the garden to dig, dig, dig!"
  (Spoken in a low chest voice)

"Out to the garden to dig, dig, dig?"
Shame on you Big Pig, Big Pig!"
  (Spoken in a light head voice)

"I'm sorry ma'am but I'm only a pig,
And all I can do is dig, dig, dig!"
  (Spoken in a low chest voice)

Author: Unknown (taken from John M. Feierabend's *First Steps in Music*. GIA Publications)

The Airplane Ride

Pitch Exploration Poem

Children respond at the end of the lines saying either "All right!" rising the second syllable with light head voice, or "Oh no!" lowering the second syllable into their low chest voice.

A man went up in an airplane. *All right!*

But the airplane didn't have an engine. *Oh, no!*

But the man had a parachute. *All right!*

But the parachute wouldn't open. *Oh, no!*

But there was a haystack under him. *All right!*

But there was pitchfork in the haystack. *Oh, no!*

But he missed the pitchfork. *All right!*

But he missed the haystack, too. *Oh, no!*

Author: John M. Feierabend, *First Steps in Music*. GIA Publications.

Props

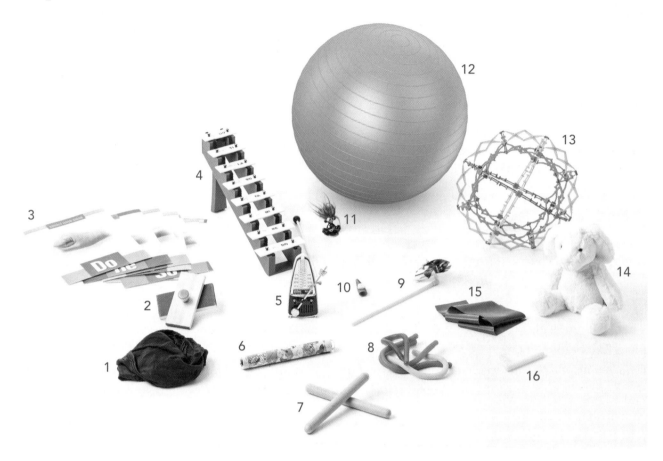

1. Scarf	9. Pinwheel
2. Sand blocks	10. Kazoo
3. Solfege flashcards	11. Small shoulder buddy
4. Step-bell instrument	12. Stability ball
5. Metronome	13. Hoberman Sphere
6. Kaleidsocope	14. Stuffed animal
7. Rhythm sticks	15. Exercise resistance band
8. Stretchy noodles	16. Straw

DANA LENTINI is passionate about teaching the art of singing to people of all ages. She began her professional work in music as a successful classical singer, but along the way she would find herself in circumstances that led her to share music with children. As someone who had been told that children shouldn't take voice lessons, Dana began an educational journey to learn about how the art and science of singing might be effectively applied to young singers. After cultivating techniques during her time teaching K-6 general music and directing children's choirs, she combined her education experiences and vocal pedagogy knowledge to create Born 2 Sing Kids, a voice program designed to nurture the development of beginning singers ages 5-13. A noted pedagogue and expert in teaching methodologies for this age group, her articles and podcasts have been distributed worldwide.

Dana holds a Bachelor of Music degree in vocal performance from the University of Southern California and a Master of Music degree in vocal pedagogy from Oakland University. In addition to her work with Born 2 Sing Kids, she has served as a member of the voice faculty in the Preparatory Department of the College Conservatory of Music (CCM) at the University of Cincinnati and in the Department of Music at The College of New Jersey. In recognition of her excellence in teaching, Dana was a 2018 recipient of the Joan Frey Boytim Award for Independent Teachers, presented by the National Association of Teachers of Singing (NATS).

When she is not teaching and writing about her studio strategies for young singers, Dana enjoys physical activities like running, yoga, and Pilates and spending time with her husband and three wonderful children, all of whom share her love of the performing arts.